Anatomy of a Collaboration

Critical Education Practice
(Vol. 6)
Garland Reference Library of Social Science
(Vol. 951)

Critical Education Practice

Shirley R. Steinberg and Joe L. Kincheloe, Series Editors

Anatomy of a Collaboration

Study of a College of Education/
Public School Partnership

Judith J. Slater

GARLAND PUBLISHING, INC.
New York & London
1996

Library of Congress Cataloging-in-Publication Data

Slater, Judith J.
    Anatomy of a collaboration : study of a college of education/
public school partnership / Judith J. Slater.
            p.   cm. — (Garland reference library of social science ; v.
951. Critical education practice ; v. 6)
        Includes bibliographical references (p.   ) and index.
        ISBN 0-8153-1644-5 (alk. paper)
            1. College-school cooperation—Florida—Dade County.
2. Florida International University. School of Education.   3. Public
schools—Florida—Dade County.   I. Title.   II. Series: Garland
reference library of social science ; v. 951.   III. Series: Garland
reference library of social science. Critical education practice ; vol. 6.
        LB2331.53.S53   1996
        378.1'03—dc20   95-51299
                                                                              CIP

Cover photograph © 1995 Edward Slater, Southern Stock Photo Agency.

Printed on acid-free, 250-year-life paper
Manufactured in the United States of America

Contents

Series Editors' Introduction

Anatomy of a Collaboration is an important book for scholars who are interested not only in collaboration between bureaucracies but also in the dynamics of bureaucratic organizations in general. Educational leaders will find the book helpful as a case study of the vicissitudes of collaborative efforts between public school bureaucracies and university teacher education organizations. Slater situates the book in the larger context of educational reform, grounding each chapter around the question: How do we overcome the intractability of bureaucracy, especially when reforms involve the collaboration of bureaucratic organizations? Using this conceptual framework, Slater delineates procedures for organizational learning—a process that recognizes the pathologies of bureaucracies so that they can be transcended by individuals seeking democratic change. In this context Slater examines Project Co-STAAR (Collaborative School to Achieve Academic Restructuring), a cooperative venture between the Dade County (Florida) schools and the College of Education at Florida International University to create a public relief school.

The essence of *Anatomy of a Collaboration* revolves around Slater's attempt to make sense of bureaucratic structures. Indeed, the book takes on the character of a bureaucratic hermeneutics, an effort to expose what is too often hidden in the daily workings of organizations. William Pinar et al. (1995) wrote that hermeneutics involves the analysis of the principles of interpretation. Such interpretation is grounded within human struggles for freedom, voice, and moral action. The importance of the hermeneutical imagination revolves around its refusal to accept hegemonic/authoritarian structures and its effort to engage them transformatively in the interpretive task. Hermeneuts are interested in questions of human meaning—how

men and women make sense of their lives, as they come to understand what has been hidden from them by layers of tradition, preju-
dice, and rationalistic procedures. As Patrick Slattery (1995) maintained, hermeneutics sets us free by providing new insights into the
world around us and our role in it. As hermeneut, Slater attempts to
free us from bureaucratic constraints by exposing the particularities
of bureaucratic tyranny.

More Than a Worthy Vision

As a student of bureaucracies, Slater contends that a vision of what
collaborative organizations could accomplish is insufficient—one
must be able to specify the interpersonal dynamics at work at the
micropolitical level of organizational behavior. Even though many
agreements were reached by the Dade County Public Schools and
Florida International University, one organization or the other would
retreat from the accords later because intrabureaucratic dynamics
prohibited particular actions. Bureaucracies are often unable to accomplish worthy political goals because they conceptually isolate
individuals operating in them to the point they lose their capacity to
empathize with the perspectives of people outside their organization. This cognitive limitation subverts the bureaucrat's ability to
imagine alternatives to present policy and to envision creative ways
of solving problems. Slater specifies the human damage that can
take place when intrabureaucratic disorders undermine cooperation
between agencies. These are not abstract theoretical ruminations,
Slater tells us, but human problems replete with painful consequences
for men, women, and children.

A Tale of Two Bureaucracies

Slater frames the public school and university bureaucracies as unique
cultural entities with different organizational structures and
micropolitical styles of self-maintenance. As hermeneut, Slater uses
semiotics to deconstruct the symbolic construction of the bureaucracies. Focusing on organizational artifacts, gender codes,
psychodynamics, and metaphors, Slater probes the organizational
Lebenswelt revealing the tacit beliefs and ideals of each "culture."
Finding two different cultures with different missions and different
assumptions, the author documents the ways in which individuals
from the organizations responded to events in a way that resonated

with the tradition of their respective agency. Thus, Slater explores the genealogies of the bureaucratic cultures, focusing on the discursive dynamics that both reflect and shape the experiences of those who work in them and those who are affected by them.

As she came to understand the unique cultures of the two bureaucracies, Slater realized how little the participants in Co-STAAR understood about the cultural differences between the two organizations. If interagency cooperation was going to work, the tale of the *two* bureaucracies had to be understood by all parties involved. The roles played by each individual in his or her organization, Slater realized, are limited and restricted in ways unknown to the other group. Bureaucratic hermeneutics, therefore, were essential to the success of the transorganization, to the attempt to break down the boundaries that separated the agencies. Operating on the basis of a constructivist epistemology, the author discerned that each participant's understanding of Co-STAAR was derived from his or her position in the web of reality in general and bureaucratic location in particular. Successful collaboration demanded that these idiosyncratic ways of seeing be negotiated by the various participants. Secret bureaucratic languages used to mystify outsiders would have to be explained in this interorganizational negotiation—a dramatic break from standard bureaucratic *modus operandi* that is too often indifferent to whether the uninitiated understand the lingo or not.

Hide and Go Seek: Authority in Bureaucracies

Even organizations that are well intentioned and committed to democratic principles, discover that their worthy goals are undermined by the everyday workings of bureaucracies. Slater understands this phenomenon, as she watched the process undermine attempts to experiment within its structures. Though public pronouncements concerning Co-STAAR were supportive, behaviors in private sometimes served to subvert such commitments. Behind the bureaucratic curtain, good intentions were squashed by the inertia of existing practice—that is, whatever a bureaucracy is presently doing (function) comes to be seen by its members as what it should be doing (purpose).

Co-STAAR demanded a change of function by both organizations. Such a demand conflicted with the maintenance of the status quo, bureaucratic stability, and existing lines of authority. The top-down hierarchies of organizations intensify tendencies for goal-displacement and rigidity. Slater and many of her cohorts operating in the middle of the hierarchy were able to view problems clearly, but were sometimes unable to convey their observations to those at the top of the pyramid in decision-making positions. Not surprisingly, authority was hidden from view. The origin of directives that obfuscated the collaboration was difficult to detect. Such realities undermined the purpose of the project and engendered tremendous frustration among those individuals dedicated to it.

Speaking of authority and its concealment, Slater tells us that the power hierarchy of organizational permission-givers in both bureaucracies was male-dominated. At the same time the middle-level negotiators were mostly female. Such realizations are often overlooked by students of bureaucracy who in their patriarchal comfort fail to notice the nakedness of the organizational leaders. It does not stretch our credulity to assert that the discourse of bureaucracy is masculine in that it abstracts (separates) us from our colleagues without setting us free. As Kathy Ferguson (1984) put it, we are isolated but not autonomous. Unlike a more feminine ethic, macho-bureaucracy binds us to specific roles and regulations rather than connecting us to other individuals. Slater is more comfortable with an experience of herself as continuous with others in the organization than with the standard bureaucratic notion of repressed affiliation. She seeks an organization that encourages its members to struggle for self-direction with one another, that validates the continual effort to synthesize the individual and the collective in a perpetual process.

Bureaucracy Produces Bureaucrats

Not only do bureaucracies *produce* bureaucrats, but they attempt to *disempower* them as well. Slater's efforts were undermined by a top-down authority that disempowered negotiators. Properly acculturated middle-level functionaries must constantly struggle with the power dynamics of their bureaucracy. Such power plays attempt to render them objects of administration, malleable personalities who are inscribed by the imprint of the organization. To maintain their dignity, they must resist in subtle ways that avoid the ire of their superiors. If such resistance fails, the subordinate must struggle to prevent the authority of the system from conflating her identity with

the organizational role she occupies. Such pressures to conform sometimes produce what Herbert Marcuse (1964) labeled "the Happy
Consciousness"—the belief that "what is" is rational and desirable
and that bureaucracies know best. If such is the case, then why not
conform? Why not please one's superiors in the larger effort to climb
the organizational ladder? Why engage in this bureaucratic
hermeneutics? Conformist pressures move one to play the subordinate role—a bit part in the bureaucratic play that discourages new
ideas or challenges to the status quo. Slater understands the ways
these ambiguous forces can undermine the organizational flexibility
needed for a transorganizational experiment like Co-STAAR.

The Bureaucratic Rationality:
The Cognitive Illness in Action

A fascinating but disturbing dehumanization process occurs in many
bureaucratic situations. The hierarchical bureaucracy creates a social
organization that interrupts human interaction and replaces it with
rationalistic roles, rules, and discourse. In this context the human
ability to empathize with other people is rationalized in a manner
that breaks empathy into several subcategories and prescribed activities. The dynamics of human exchange are codified into a set
of procedures and, as a result, authenticity and autonomy are undermined. Bureaucrats must make a concerted effort to overcome
such tendencies in their daily affairs in the organizational culture.
Such ways of operating constitute part of a larger phenomenon I
have referred to elsewhere as the *cognitive illness* of Cartesian-
Newtonian rationalism (Kincheloe, 1993, 1995). The cognitive illness restricts our social imagination as it fragments the world to the
point that we are unable to see human experience as a connected
whole. Attempting to study the world in isolation, bit by bit, experts have separated education, psychology, and social analysis from
the culture that produced such ways of seeing. For the purpose of
simplifying the process of analysis, these disciplines of study are divided arbitrarily without regard for larger context.

The fragmented thinking symptomatic of the cognitive illness
weakens our ability to see relationships between our actions and the
world. As we come to value autonomy over participation, isolation
over communion, we begin to view the natural world and the hu-

mans who live in it as objects for exploitation and manipulation. If we continue to isolate and analyze the various aspects of the world of humans, we come to justify their manipulation and control in the name of science and efficiency. A bureaucratic hermeneutics intervenes in this form of thinking. Slater addresses some of these issues, maintaining that the bureaucratic propensity for centralized control, task specialization, accountability, and internal standardization works to compartmentalize knowledge. Such compartmentalization and standardization subvert attempts of bureaucracies to learn about their own problems and to see beyond their interoffice memos. Power and ideological implications of the work of the bureaucracy are erased—without knowledge of internal problems and the political/ideological effects of the organization, the process of learning is stifled. Slater witnessed the results of this process in her observations of collaborative process.

Beyond Understanding: The Possibility of Resistance

Slater is interested in the question of the role of leadership in bureaucratic change. Transformative leaders must look beyond the attempt to change individuals to fit the organization. In a democratic context, leaders must connect concern with the individual with the larger socio-political context in which the bureaucracy operates. In the discourse of American politics, the pathology of bureaucratization has been denounced regularly by office seekers and incumbents alike; the talk is cheap, however, as little effort has been directed in the political arena to understanding and changing bureaucracies—either public or private. To operate in a manner Slater would approve, bureaucracies must be changed from within their ranks. Individuals operating alone are much too vulnerable to retribution by their superiors to accomplish the palace coup—a large number of united men and women working together can provide the mutual support and protection needed to engineer a velvet revolution within the bureaucratic order. Transformative leaders in this asphyxiating situation would require the ability to read and expose power relationships, to support the efforts of the bureaucratic functionaries to overcome their fear of their superiors, and to expose the dehumanization processes that members have come to consider the normal workings of the agency. No bureaucracy is powerful enough to control all manifestations of opposition. Thus, the power to resist the organization and its inflexibility always exists.

Understanding the problems of contemporary organizations delineated in this book, individuals working in and affected by bureaucracies can begin to formulate an alternative set of values on which to ground the organizations of the future. New, more spiritual understandings of personal identity and interpersonal relations will help guide workers in their efforts to identify hegemonic spaces around which resistance can be organized. Antibureaucratic organizations that are decentralized rely on authentic human-to-human relationships rather than authoritarian edicts, are democratic not simply stratified, and appreciate the value of sharing, not hoarding, information. Kathy Ferguson (1984) argued that such antibureaucracies are more concerned with process than outcome and view power as something used to enable members to accomplish as a group what they couldn't accomplish separately. *Anatomy of a Collaboration* is the story of the efforts of a group of educators to establish an important educational institution and the organizational obstacles they encountered along the way. Slater believes that collaborative, community-based solutions to educational challenges are necessary. The rocky road to those solutions is mapped here for the benefit of future travelers.

Joe L. Kincheloe
Shirley R. Steinberg

References

Ferguson, K. (1984). *The Feminist Case Against Bureaucracy*. Philadelphia: Temple University Press.

Kincheloe, J. (1993). *Toward a Critical Politics of Teacher Thinking: Mapping the Postmodern*. Westport, CT: Bergin and Garvey.

Kincheloe, J. (1995). *Toil and Trouble: Good Work, Smart Workers, and the Integration of Academic and Vocational Education*. New York: Peter Lang.

Pinar, W., W. Reynolds, P. Slattery, and P. Taubman (1995). *Understanding Curriculum*. New York: Peter Lang.

Marcuse, H. (1964). *One Dimensional Man*. Boston: Beacon Press.

Slattery, P. (1995). *Curriculum Development in the Postmodern Era*. New York: Garland Publishing.

Introduction

This book is an essay on collaboration. It is based on empirical and qualitative data—largely participant observation—of a lengthy process of reform and discovery. It examines two organizations and the people who work in them, and then explores the possibilities of collaboration between them.

The goal of this work is to critically examine the process and the conditions that allow for success and failure of reform. The reform effort revolved around the collaboration of two organizations to design and develop an elementary school from the ground up. These two organizations had a history of operating in parallel within the same community, taking from and sharing with each other only what was necessary for the individual and often personal goals of each. The reform was geared toward whether this mode of operation within each organization, which relied primarily on stasis to service a large urban school system, could evolve into a structure in which the influence, ideals and innovations in design, operation, curriculum and instruction, delivery, and support are altered from the habitual. Analysis of the process of moving away from the past was undertaken through a critical examination of the elements, both personal and public, that permit and deter a collaboration from occurring as well as the paradigms and metaphors from the literature on organizations, change, and leadership, and even literature itself with relevant applications to public schools and colleges of education. Further, this analysis is of the people who, through their presence and influence, were able to introduce and support new ways of working. What was traditional for each organization had to be balanced with what was proposed as innovative in operation and design for the new school. The synergy of ideas from people who understand how each parent organization works offered opportunities for a new model of interaction to emerge.

The College of Education of Florida International University and Dade County Public Schools entered into a long-range planning effort to design, build, and operate a public elementary relief school on the university's main campus. The analysis of this collaborative effort of representatives from both organizations—the initiation, negotiation, and compromises that occurred—is but one part of the story. The other, more crucial aspect is whether two different organizations—one a bureaucratic top-down structure with assigned roles, responsibilities, and postures and the other a loosely defined, entrepreneurial, informally driven structure—can collaborate at all.

Interviews, in situ diagnosis, participant observation, and qualitative analysis of the two-year process of negotiations are used to describe the anatomy of the collaboration. Analysis of organizational climate, political motivation, lines of authority, pressure to conform, resistance to change, and leadership theory will be part of the exploration of whether the two organizations can share or create a transformative vision.

Organizational Operations

Most of the literature on leadership, organizational change, and planning comes from business, management, and leadership theory. In education, we may embrace the theoretical and adopt an ideology, but implementing through practice is often met with resistance by participants and sometimes leads to conscious and unconscious subversion of goals. The present looks more like the past than like preparation for the future. Attempts at empowerment in education and professionalization have met with mixed or little success in the public schools. Therefore, when presented with opportunities to make radical change, to break the mold, to explore new structures and take risks, to implement research, to open doors, or to dialogue with the very organizations that prepare their future workers, participants have a tendency to reinforce the walls and boundaries that protect the framework of the familiar and defend its very existence.

This is true of both the university and the school system. Each in its own way protects itself and maintains itself and the culture in which the players operate. If colleges of education hope to make a difference and influence politically powerful public school systems, the interaction cannot be one of imposition of one point of view over the other. Instead, we need to look at ourselves as a new kind of society—one that forges new linkages, works with the school system to create reasoned alternatives, and helps the public school system evaluate itself through a trusting atmosphere of collaboration.

This analysis was undertaken with the following assumptions and limitations: As a trained observer in the area of instructional leadership, the author represents a tradition of analysis of curricular orientation that views social interaction as a reflection of cognitive structures and personal perceptual orientation. People act in ways consonant with their own views of possibilities for action in a constructed phenomenological world of their own making. Impediments to reform and resistance to change must be overcome by the remaking of the individual's perceptual field through strategies of reeducation as described by the work of Kurt Lewin. This story of collaboration is limited by the author's own perception of the meanings and interpretations of the educative process during the three years of negotiation. The value system utilized in this analysis is a reflection of the author's own point of view and the belief that the position represented by each organization at the beginning of the process is not where each should be at the end. Visionary? Yes! Possible? Maybe! What makes each organization move forward, and why should the organizations move forward in a direction that crosses paths? That is the reeducative strategy and the goal of the process from the author's side of the negotiations, at least.

The language used to describe the process of planned change has sources in a multiplicity of disciplines. In an effort to be precise in description, we often succumb to using Wittgenstein's language game—the use of words that have undisputable meaning for the collective. Recognizing that this is almost impossible to achieve, let me describe my interpretation of the "dogs of change." When asked to recollect "dog," most people think of a particular dog—a poodle, a great dane, or the like. Asked to list the characteristics of "dog," the category—the universals—the academic task becomes one in which we describe the criteria for collective understanding. Yet, we persist in applying our own interpretation to the word based on our unique experience and acculturation to the world. Within each organization particular, unique metaphors and analogies represent "dog" even though both organizations exist within one profession. Therefore, often I will use terms that are described and understood by one organization in very different ways from the ways they are by the other. The only way we understand each other's contextual truth about a term is the evidence and feedback observed through the way people operate and act upon their own understanding, that is, their own point of view.

When all the analysis and data are presented, we must recognize that organizations have goals congruent with their missions as stated and understood by the people who work in them. Sometimes the overriding goal is one of preserving the organization itself at the expense of the mission. Attempts at change are specks upon the landscape described by the formal organizational structure. Like the transformed and ignored character in Kafka's *Metamorphosis*, people don't look clearly or notice the changes around them while they are attending to the details of daily life. Individuals may become less important, or even be ignored, living in the midst of the organization's effort to produce observable, measurable products. Planned changes may have fleeting influence; as in García Marquez's *One Hundred Years of Solitude*, everything may return to the way it was before as the jungle swallows up all innovation when people no longer make an effort to keep the forces of nature at bay.

Lastly, the author believes, like Konig (1968, I), in the value of a shared *Gemeinde*, or local community life and existence. The point of commonality is not in organizational and administrative authority, but in a social reality and relationships that could promote organic growth that sweeps along both organizations. The wants and needs of an individual (in this case one organization or one person within an organization) must fall in line with the total operation. The problem, then, is how to accomplish this so that the result is a biotic community (Konig, 1968, 8–11) of human associations. The community is a culture, and people create that culture by recognizing that the totality is a social system unto itself. Players have a social identity, and they form social relationships and limitations consciously. The *Mr. Roger's Neighborhood* theme song says that "it's a beautiful day in this neighborhood," but who determines what constitutes a beautiful day? Konig (1968, 129) said that integration, or the linking by common bonds both horizontally and vertically, adds to the creation and unity of direction of this biotic community.

How is this done? Possibly through Etzioni's (1993) communitarianism, the popularist view that there are shared values and institutions that support them. This view looks at community as a web of social bonds that allows us to speak as one, but with this comes responsibility for individuals and institutions, such as colleges and school districts. Special interest groups represent imposition, whereas freedom for individuals requires the community (Etzioni, 1993, 15).

Like Rousseau's social contract, the real question is one of freedom: What are the conditions that allow individuals to live, work, and prosper in a collective while collaborating to optimize freedom for all? Clearly this project showed that a balance needs to be achieved between the public and private perceptions, open and closed contexts, personal and public goals, and public and personal commitment. Greene (1988, xi) asserted that the search for a dialectic of freedom is a search for freedom in dialogue with others. "The aim is to find (or create) an authentic public space. . . . Such a space requires the provision of opportunities for the articulation of multiple perspectives in multiple idioms, out of which something common can be brought into being. It requires, as well, a consciousness of the normative as well as of the possible: of what *ought* to be, from a moral and ethical point of view, and what is in the making, what *might* be in an always open world" (Greene, 1988, xii).

Freedom, then, is collaboration without pretense, which is nurtured, informed, and communally sustained (Greene, 1988, 43). Individuals only have to come together in a particular way and be authentic with one another in a project they mutually pursue. Of course, authentic to Greene is doing away with pretense, badges of authority, and masks of titles (Greene, 1988, 16).

This project, then, is the story of change versus tradition, of perceptions versus reality, of community versus individual power. This view of the process and the ensuing analysis represent the author's bias of perception, if you will. The story is intriguing, nevertheless.

Summary of Chapters

The first chapter of this book directs the reader to explore the conditions within schools that perpetuate the status quo. What aspect of the operation and practice of schools perpetuates the familiar while appearing to be in the midst of reform? Part of the answer lies in lack of clarity of goals. Where we want to go, where we have come from, and critically determining what the steps are to achieve individual vision—let alone collective vision—is not an easy course to run. Perhaps clues to solving many of the problems associated with schools lie in what we have achieved successfully in the past. The dissolution of communities and lack of full participation of the stakeholders have created real impediments to reform efforts. These also have insulated systemic efforts to make change.

Chapter 2 presents an overview of the methodology used for analysis of organizational structure in this study. Analysis of the two organizations presented in the case study includes power/authority, norms/standards, cohesion/morale, goals/objectives, and structure differentiation in operation. The differences in worldviews held by each organization become apparent when the perspective of organizational culture is the unit of analysis. Aspects of organizational culture include the ecological context in which participants engage, the formal and informal rules within which they operate, the critical historical forces that regulate individual behavior, and the social, demographic expectations held for each other.

It is posited that what is needed for this project to succeed, given the differences that exist between the two organizations, is for each to develop the capacity to learn, to move forward, to create new mental models of what a collaboration could mean. The sharing of a new vision is possible if each recognizes the patterns of behavior and beliefs that undermine learning and growth.

Chapter 3 presents the history and context of the project using a semiotic approach of description for the process, events, words, behaviors, and objects that carry meaning for members of the two communities. Trends that influenced the decision to pursue a collaboration between a public school and a college of education include America 2000, Blueprint 2000 (a Florida initiative), and the movement toward privatization, local control, and a booming influx of students in a majority minority environment. An overview of empirical-rational, normative reeducative, and power-coercive change strategies provides the theoretical base to look at the individuals in both organizations and the interventions employed to control the project.

A description of the process of the project from early formal and informal meetings through subcommittee work between counterparts from the two organizations is presented in Chapter 4. Team building, consensual differences, attempts at domination, and rewards for involvement are described qualitatively and metaphorically.

Because organizations are always in motion, this project at times was in step and at other times out of step with other activities. Although agreement was reached on issues that emerged, often one side or the other backed off at a later date because the idea was not institutionalized and could not exist within the context of past and present events or trends. What are the conditions, then, that can create culture, and what kind of leadership is necessary to make a transactional endeavor transformative in product?

Chapter 5 describes the complications and intricacies of negotiation as a juggling act between reinforcing and stabilizing the people and events. The process is fraught with rumors and half truths, circles of influence outside the negotiations, and intergroup dynamics that can make or break good intentions. People espouse values they can't or won't ever implement.

The negotiation phase is described in terms of information flow, public and private information, conflict resolution strategies, and control. Continuing throughout this project was the struggle for power and domination by one organization over the other. This mode of operation, largely structurally based and typical of bureaucratic structures, had to be meliorated by a group of people who could move beyond the structural limitations and create an environment of trust and mutual support.

Chapter 6 looks at resistance to change and the "I don't want to play anymore, especially by your rules, so I'm taking my toys home" syndrome. Sharing the burden of work includes sharing the responsibility for success or the blame for failure.

What happens when resistance to change is for good reasons? I suspect that the school system viewed each of the following as good reasons not to change: maintenance of the system and lines of authority; a belief that the way they operate is the correct way; distrust that the other side's position can't accomplish the goals and objectives of the organization; history of past failures; and unreliability of follow-through in people not directly under the organization's authority. The question is whether the college can facilitate the development of a new identity and change at least the outside perception of its own culture to help overcome external resistance and whether we can have transformative leadership in educational endeavors; whether we can share a vision, let alone create one. Can the resultant plan ensure improvement? Can either organization engage in long-range planning, or does each merely cope, react, and maintain? What, then, are the conditions that create culture, and what leadership is needed to support and maintain it?

The final proposal is analyzed by comparing the product to the formative needs, goals, objectives of the project. The final proposal is a compromise that transforms the ideas of the subcommittees into practice and then is screened by the special interests of each organization. Chapter 7 evaluates the changes in each organization from completion of the written proposal and plans for the building, staffing, and governance of the school. What are the indicators of success in the aftermath of this project? How have the spheres of influence in each organization been changed by this project? Can the innovation outlast the leadership of each organization?

Chapter 8 is a call for advancing community solutions for a redefined school community. The complexity of schooling in communities that are changing and evolving requires participation and support from universities that prepare teachers, from school districts that introduce teachers to new roles specific to the environment in which they work, and from the larger community of which these institutions are a part. Working together, the players can envision and create a future that is more humane and responsive to the needs and desires of all members.

Finally, Chapter 9 is an analysis of what I set out to accomplish by narrating the story of this collaborative effort and what remains to be learned through organizational research. The issues and concerns of leadership, organizational behavior, team membership, problem solving, communication, and resolution of conflict are discussed so that others wishing to participate in collaborative efforts are aware of the costs and the benefits. Creating and sustaining a true collaboration between organizations is not the norm in education, but the failure of systemic reform among schools and universities in the past necessitates the evolution of structures and vehicles for authentic dialogue and action for the future. I hope that this book helps to move that process forward through a mutual restructuring of traditional roles that is more responsive to our changing environment.

The Parable

As a participant observer in the process of negotiating the collaboration of a new public elementary school on the campus of the university in which I work, I was constantly reminded of a play titled *A Walk in the Woods*. The setting is Geneva; the purpose, nuclear arms control negotiation. The two main characters, a Russian and an American, have a public persona that separates them by a gulf of culture, history, politics, and role expectations. The newly appointed American negotiator is taken for a walk in the woods by the seasoned Russian negotiator, not to talk about arms and private deals, as the American would like, but to talk about life, to tell jokes, and to look at the foliage. The formal negotiations, the Russian explains, are "the quest for the appearance for the quest for peace" and not peace itself or progress toward any goal. It is the impression that they are negotiating—looking for peace and never really finding it— that they give to the outside world, until, as we now know, history changed the politics and culture of Russia in the summer of 1991.

At the end of the play, spring has come and flowers are beginning to bloom. The Russian tells the American that he will now have to negotiate with someone else who is replacing him. The American is distraught and cajoles the Russian to remain. "Friends share hope!" the American says. "I am your friend," says the Russian. He will leave and the process will begin again with new players, but these two have changed each other. They have come to some personal understanding at an individual level that transcends the organizations in which they operate. Maybe that alone constitutes success.

Chapter One
The Ready-to-Wear School

Schools are built beautifully today. I live and work in an area where new construction abounds, where new schools are visions of the possible—clean, architecturally pleasing, a mirage of art deco colors, glass, and open spaces that complement the weather and lifestyle. Older schools have been renovated, and they too are technologically savvy places, filled with the environmental trappings of modern, if not postmodern, education. But, upon closer examination, there is a striking similarity to them. This is a familiarity that transcends the design and equipment. This is the commonplace of schools that makes them more similar than they are different, that gives the viewer the perception that the same things are going on inside and propels the vision of quality as being the common milieu. They come in different sizes and different shapes with different students inside, but the mode of operation, the presentation, and the range of variety from one to the other is hauntingly familiar. This sameness is not accidental. It serves a purpose as old as schools. It helps replicate the cultural understandings and beliefs that are the very fabric of our society. It transmits the cultural heritage and reproduces those elements that are deemed most valuable by those who make policy and are in positions of decision-making power. It, in effect, dissuades huge variation and redirection of purpose, even when experimentation is supported and change is in the air.

Schools today are structurally like the clothing industry's ready-to-wear collection, which mimics the designer's one of a kind. The majority of us who can't afford to purchase the designer clothes go to the mall, to a chain store, or to a discount outlet (the modern form of getting a deal!). Each store carries the same merchandise, different sizes, all off the rack, and we have convinced ourselves that we are not only getting the exact same product as the designer model, but also that this is desirable that everyone make their choices from this limited version and menu. We are at the mercy of the copier of the designer goods. The copier takes what is apparent on the outside and duplicates the product to look like the original, but the stitching, the details, the uniqueness, and the quality of the finished product are different from the original. The copy, because it isn't made as well as the original, doesn't wear as well. The advertisement tells us they are the same, but advertisers shape public opinion and don't support critical awareness. Advertisers make us think we are getting an exact duplicate of the "best" when what we are getting is only a poor imitation.

Schools that duplicate successes from other places look the same as the copied designer clothes. Worse, they often look like last year's clothes, as the last bastion of replication of something successful is perpetuated long after it has outlived its usefulness and appropriateness. We see ourselves walking down the street and confirm that what we wear is appropriate, new, and current. We have it all! Except it is not current and not appropriate. It was created for another population, another setting, by those who are not familiar with our unique needs. And, what if our needs are changing all the time, as is the case in Miami and other areas where the population changes daily and dramatically? How do we remain current, fashionable, and responsive to a future that is not so clearly described? Who speaks for us, the teachers and researchers, about best practice and shared commitment to research and innovation, when our standards are created by those outside the profession? Have we lost our voice, lost our opinion, and allowed the popular to form our taste?

I have this vision of the creation of a school that looks less like the others, that meets the individualistic needs of the student population it serves, that is not hampered by someone else's vision of what is appropriate, but instead is allowed to be created by a process that frees itself from the restrictions and assumptions that what works for one is good for all. This place allows all stakeholders to participate fully. It allows anyone concerned with the welfare and good of the school and the community it serves and the students who attend to have the opportunity to create something specific, good, and just for the people who live and work there. It allows for the collective vision and voice of participants, and it creates a positive outlook and tenor for the possible. It is a community of those concerned with the quality and care of the students who attend. This community is free of the political constraints and bureaucratic entanglements that restrict the possible from becoming a reality. It is a positive environment in which excuses for why you "can't" do something are turned into synergistic dialogue to promote the "can."

Why is this unusual? Why is this not the norm? Is this not in the realm of the work of the professional in schools? I have worn many hats and played many roles in my career. I have been a teacher for multiple grade levels; I have explored the possibility and stretch of creative imagination as a teacher of gifted students for many years. I have been a parent advocate, department chair, head of the faculty, and union representative, sometimes for protection of myself and others who saw things differently and were not content with the status quo. Sometimes seeing things in different ways is dangerous, even if the end result is good for students and community. Sometimes you have to protect yourself and others in order to vision the future. The past, and past practices, are much easier to rely on and perpetuate. The past has a map.

Some fundamental questions must be addressed in any effort to make change within schools: What are our goals for educating the youth? What are our desires for them? We have to be very clear because much of what is current may, in fact, be incompatible when implemented simultaneously. Current reforms have a tendency to negate each other. The scramble for experimentation—duplication of successes from one site to another or from one community to another—assumes that structural changes result in similar outcomes. This perpetuates the belief that scientific proof can be generalized, even if that science is pseudoscientific and applied uniformly across the board without regard for individual uniqueness of location. What is the criteria for selection of reform? It may be something inherent in what we believe is good and just and right for all children. It could be more specific; if so, if the stakeholders are in agreement, we should be able to forge ahead to accomplish the goals. This doesn't happen often in practice since each of the stakeholders belongs to a larger organization that is bound by a culture that operates both formally and informally. Each of these organizations has implicit and explicit understandings and beliefs that guide their operation and create the uniformity of behaviors and position viewed by outsiders as the norm.

Let us suppose that the diversity present within and between organizations can be understood and work can go forward with this knowledge. If goals then can be collectively determined and articulated, the reality is that each organization involved understands them still through their own lens of meaning. That which is collectively determined may from beginning to end be understood and implemented individualistically by those who make up the community. This is a philosophically based orientation that must be understood. Goals and decisions for implementation may be geared to perpetuate the culture and status quo of the group that is dominant or the one that has within its possession the power, control, and structure to direct decision making toward their own purposes. If so, the future may look more like the past than the reform efforts set out to accomplish.

The reverse scenario is one in which the organizations involved can come to agreement about making change, and power and control are shared in an idealistic forum characterized by a genuine exchange of ideas and opportunities. What then are the responsibilities and who takes the initiative for each part of the process of implementation? Do some people and their parent organizations have to give anything up for success to occur? Are their losses tangible and real or internal and harder to abandon? How are these people seen by their colleagues? Do they think they have abandoned the mission and goals of their own organization, or worse, are they now exhibiting behaviors that look more like those of the enemy? How do individuals protect themselves from these accusations while empowered to create changes that may benefit all in the long run?

We have to make decisions about our very beliefs as a collective and as individuals within the collective as to what is good and just and fair. We have lost sight of the purpose of schooling. Reforms are at the mercy of business, technology, national priorities, and domination of interest groups rather than being focused on helping children and families. Many parents give up their child to the school and believe that the school will do the best for them. They do not question the authority of the school; they do not know to become involved, ask questions, and understand the process of schooling so that their child can benefit from the experience. If their child is not successful, they blame the child because they believe in the authority of the school and would not dare to question the school's intent.

This paradox of sorts has led to the reliance on technological solutions to help create responses to school problems. This has not proved fruitful either. We cannot use or rely on the belief, popular in modern culture, that we can have a technological solution to humanistic problems. Technology provides the opportunity for alternatives. It has not been and will not be the solution to a changing field of demands placed on education. It has provided a theory about teaching and learning, of teacher preparation, and the standardization of process, but the raw materials respond more uniquely than technology is able to predict. The technology itself has become subservient to the mechanization it creates. The mechanical aspects take on a life of their own as they become the ends of the process and success is determined by how well the mechanization works. Is it efficient, of quality, well implemented, documentable? This doesn't work in schools because of people—people who are teachers, who come with their own beliefs, experiences, and backgrounds, and people who are students who come from a diversity of environments and cultures—and governmental restrictions. The technology has detoured schools from the humanistic mission they were created to serve.

We used to create schools that were part of communities. Children rode their bikes to school, neighbors watched them, and the community was responsible for each other. Now, we have disintegrated neighborhoods, and we have replaced the normative environment with a technology of school that, in theory, would serve that function, but, in practice, is devoid of the essence of the people that inhabit and support it. Technology is prescriptive also. If a child comes to school hungry, the way to solve the problem is to diagnose and prescribe. The source of the problem is not part of the solution finding. As problems change, schools respond with technological methods of finding solutions. Modernization is technologically driven, but practice has not kept up with the changing nature of the cultural mix. The blueprints for solutions are for problems that are long gone.

Collaboration as Ideal

This project sought to create something new and collaborative between a public school system and a university. It attempted to provide for an operating structure that was detached from the political,
social life of the parent institutions, thus creating a freer working
atmosphere. Free, however, means to be loosened from that which
you find restrictive or self-perpetuating at the expense of or limitation of the new. Not everyone who participated in this project was
on a quest for the humanistic freedom to participate fully. Some
were, instead, interested in seeing everyone buy in to the existing
structures and patterns of operation because they truly believed that
the present methods are the best. To actively be free from the restrictions, you must first be aware of what they are. The fight has always
been between that habitual mode of operating and living within a
culture that maintains and perpetuates itself and the waves of reform that seek to make change. The maintenance is accomplished
through the very political and social aspects of a culture that perpetuates processes that dominate and characterize its functions. To
collectively work toward a reachable future, we must have the desire
to change first, and then, secondly, we must have an understanding
of what we want to change from.

In the case of this project, what was seen as an opportunity to
change was the interaction between two organizational cultures. This
culture is operationalized over time through the established behaviors supported by very distinct belief systems that nourish the abilities of each respective staff member to be successful. Collectively
this creates the identity of each organization as understood by the
people who work within each culture. As this project unfolded, it
became increasingly difficult to distinguish what elements of operation were liberating and what elements were perpetuating and resistant to change. Often what seemed to be liberating, in practice, was
too loosely coupled to create the conditions for true, lasting change.

Part of the problem is that culture is tied so intimately with our
technological growth and competitiveness that we cannot hope to
change it without undermining the very structure that supports its
perpetuation. This is clearly evident in school. Any time teachers are
asked to make a change, they react with a great deal of resistance.

Why? Are they resisting the innovation or are they protecting the last vestige of their own personal freedom, which reflects beliefs perhaps not consistent with the change? What do we require of them? That they be modern, that they align with progress, that they act in ways that are clearly inconsistent with the beliefs they hold about their identity within the organization. All of this is forced in the name of progress, as we demand that people act in ways that they cannot believe in.

Transitions must be established to create bridges to something different (Dewey, 1939). We must find new ways of operation, new understandings, and new reactions to build successfully an environment that is being created anew. Otherwise, there is resistance to what appears to be totalitarian control, and, as Dewey stated (10), that control is not just over actions, but includes feelings, emotions, desires, and opinions as people are told what to think, how to act, and how they will be measured and rated in concordance with these measures of success. There really is no objective test, however, for whether people believe in what they are asked to do or why they persist in not complying without discord. The dominant form of behavior is an affect of the culture of the organization, and this creates the boundaries of what is possible, the ideas people have about their individuality, their worldview, and their conscious rationalizations.

A delicate relationship exists between the organization and its culture and the society and political democracy within which the organization operates. Some motivations from without the organization are significant influences through the economic, political, aesthetic, scientific, or some other self-interest wielding of power that impacts on whether the organization is adaptable to become freer in the way it conducts its business (Dewey, 1939, 17). "Individuals can find the security and protection that are prerequisites for freedom only in association with others—and then the organization these associations take on, as a measure of securing their efficiency, limits the freedom of those who have entered into them" (Dewey, 1939, 166). Dewey used the term *organization* as synonymous with association and society! Individuality demands that the association develop, sustain itself, and arrange and coordinate its elements; otherwise, it is formless and void of power. When power limits the opportunity to create, however, it limits the very freedom it was designed to enhance.

What are the conditions of freedom that would create the opportunities for individuals and organizations to operate for the benefit of the community of school? How do we create the conditions necessary for the opportunity to be adaptive and responsive to a changing field? I think the clues lie in the freedom and individuality of people who live, work, and have a stake in the community rather than in group or organizational solutions. This requires cooperation, a natural component of communities that perhaps we have lost or destroyed as our mission became misdirected toward the cultural reproduction of what was artificially created at the expense of real community. Have we lost, as Dewey predicted, democracy whose "home is the neighborly community" (1939, 159)? Rules, regulations, legal restrictions, control over the body politic, all pose limitations on community. These limitations were not part of the economic reasons for the natural associations of community life Dewey saw as a forum and platform for communication of emotions, ideas, and joint collaboration (159). Even in 1939, Dewey cautioned about ready-made intellectual goods that would come with ready-made food, articles of clothing, and gadgets, all of which distance the individual from a personal share in the manufacture of the very things we learn to value (46). It is like attending an art festival, where we marvel at the people who make things by hand and look less at the quality of their products. The marvel is their ability to not produce the ready-to-wear that has become our habitus. If we are to serve the newly emerging community—ethnically diverse, politically changing, with students coming from other lands who have lived under different beliefs and conditions of existence with life habits formed that are different from those here—do we perpetuate the commonplace of our institutions? Rather, maybe those institutions need to embrace new directions and simplify (74).

Creating an Atmosphere of Community

The creation of community is like the creation of an artistic product, or as Michelangelo wrote, analogous to divine creation. The process is more important to the enduring qualities of the work than the finished creation because we can educate people to appreciate. Truly creative, original products are produced with the condition of leaving past practices and sensibilities behind. Thus, the public and the buyer need to come to appreciate them and understand them, and that is the problem with new replacing old models of taste.

This is not very different from my life working in schools for over twenty years. Many changes came and went, but they were structural changes, not qualitative changes. Recent innovations, such as year-round schools and uniforms, are sold to the public with assurances that the traditional measures of success—grades, scores, and normative comparisons—will be affected and most certainly will go up as a result. But, what is the relationship of each to the evaluation measures, and are these attempts creating systemic changes in our sensibilities and understandings of the way change evolves?

There is an intrigue with moving from the present reality to the ideal vision. This intrigue involves the personal decision making that subverts purpose as each person tries to protect his or her own organization or the position he or she occupies within that organization. The idea that working together may be more effective to meet the needs of students and families, or at least be more efficient, does not seem to be compelling enough. Doubt is always cast as to motivation and attempts at control. While working in a local school district, I took a parent and her child for a psychological evaluation. This family had many problems, and they had learned to deal with the system with anger and distrust. The effort to get this far was enormous. I had to sit, talk, and cajole both the mother and child to get them to go to and then stay for the evaluation. Did the child need to be evaluated? Yes. I truly believe so, but the system does not recognize how threatening this can be even to families that cry out with critical needs, both emotional and physical. There is a mystery to the mask of professionalization that is not only hard for parents to understand, but also is not even respectful to other professionals from supposedly supporting fields. I sat in the house while they got ready. I drove them there. I sat in the room for the intake interview, and I sat there in the waiting room as both the mother and son were evaluated. I was there as we toured the full-time school facility where he was referred for a full-time program to meet his needs. I sat there next to the parent as she was told that she would have to sign away permission to medicate as a condition of entrance into this program because this was the right place for her son. They had not told her this and they had not told me this either, until the day of the staffing. I sat there as she got up and somehow found a way to escape with her son and herself and no car and no money, but she got back home and would be forever more furious at a system that did not help her or any of her children—blame, blame, blame. She learned to trust no one, ever, from this experience, even those who mean well, myself included; trust no one, because the situation may not be what it seems. Was she wrong? In the mechanistic solution to problems, the system protects itself by putting on a mask of superiority that its solutions are the only solutions. The system protects itself and in the process loses the humanity that it was intended to serve.

Even when there is less system structure to hamper the innovation, there is doubt and distrust of motivation and intent. Take from the giver and keep the cultures apart, shrouded in mystery. I was in college in the sixties. It was a time when each new experience was valid and the quest for knowledge was not bound by the formality of schoolhouse walls. Every Saturday I went to teach art in a storefront in Bed-Sty (the Bed-Sty I loved as the home to the Brooklyn Dodgers until they left in '57, the date no self-respecting Brooklynite would ever forget). This was the same Bed-Sty where prospective teachers would later be trained to meet the ever more complex needs of inner-city youth. Each Saturday I got off the train and made my way, fearless, to the neighborhood storefront. Clyde, my future protector, elementary-school aged, came in and adopted me; he would walk me from then on each week to the train. Somehow he knew which train I would be taking, and he would walk me to the storefront as well to keep me safe. He was my protector from the neighborhood that didn't want strangers there; he was my protector from the unknown that could occur but wouldn't as long as he was by my side. Once he did protect me, by pushing me into a closet at the back of the store. I never learned from what I was being protected, but I knew why—to keep the program alive! It had less to do with me than the service being provided. There was no personal connection involved in this interchange of goods and services. It was a business deal, nonemotional and practical. It had a purpose and goal devoid of human interaction and individual mission.

Teaching is also typically noncollaborative in nature. Cooperation is unusual; collaboration is even more so. My experience in schools brings me to the conclusion that the structural organization and roles assumed by participants are not conducive to collaboration, let alone partnerships. This is because of the fragmentation and alienation produced by schools, which isolate teachers from each other. Teachers are the front line to the community the school serves. They are inculcated with behaviors that are the norm that do not allow the sharing to take place that would support collaboratives. For example, when I started teaching there was a wave of reform called the Trump Plan, which basically was the team teaching model. I worked in an older school where the buildings were old and crowded. I taught in a recycled building, and the "stuff" (large open spaces with shared equipment and physical resources) needed to implement teaming simply was not available, and the county would not invest in a site without these trappings. But, my friends and I were intent that physical space would not restrict us. We decided, and convinced our principal, that we could team—all six of us—in the configuration we had. So, we teamed and it worked. A parent would come in, and six teachers would meet for a conference and be able to tell the parent about their child's strengths and where and how we were providing additional support and skills for the child to be successful. We instituted flexibility of placement and individualized instruction. We did so in a Korean War army barracks turned into a classroom. We wanted the innovation and the collegiality, but physically, we were not in a school that was selected for the experiment. The organization lost out, but we persisted and that year I taught fourth graders to graph quadratic equations with two unknowns because I finished the year's work by winter break. I did not know about Dewey then. I only knew that what we were doing was good for the students and good for the community that we tried to establish. No one else at the site tried it, however. No one else embraced our vision or was willing to try.

The current rhetoric of reform merely asks to change the face of U.S. education. It asks to build the school and assumes the innovations, like teaming, will follow. It doesn't require that the heart be touched. The constant redirection, or directing back, toward goals and mission without regard for the daily life of children and their families disregards what is possible. It moves the family further away from the focus of reform and from those trying to support and sustain them. To be closer to those whom we wish to support, the nature of communities has to change and an integral part of that is to have responsive schools that also are community-building models for the larger community.

I want a change in personal vision, an atmosphere of a democratic community school collaboration where individual views merge and are directed toward alignment. This process is slow to occur because of the long time needed to change the very beliefs that people hold. My vision stems from my educational experience. I guess I was blessed with an unusual education. I went to a high school that now is over two hundred years old. It is the second oldest high school in the country, and my memories of it are of more than place. It had a culture and a sensibility that was actively transmitted to me through the environment, structure, and standards that were overtly transmitted and inadvertently provided by the presence of the tradition all around me. It was something intangible yet culture building and supportive, shared by staff, administration, and students. It was a cloak of protection we shared that allowed each person to strive to be their best. It was not housed in the modern trappings of the ready-to-wear school, but in a tradition of excellence that permeated this school. This feeling of place was more than the building; it was something I didn't and don't feel in other schools, especially the ready-to-wear, off-the-rack school that doesn't understand why the building of community is so hard and yet so essential. No one "graffitied" that school then as they do now. No one could imagine that even as a possibility. The creation of community meant that the community was for everyone and therefore was protected by everyone and advanced by everyone. The school took the adolescents and did what school was supposed to do; it helped develop the forming bodies and minds by a unified vision and behaviors that created a reality of the possible as an achievable goal, and in doing so sustained the community of support.

The discourse of communities can be the success of communities. The dialogue opens individuals to those possibilities. The questions asked may be different from place to place and time to time, but it is the local issues that are the subject of the dialogue. And, the discourse must be genuine for results to be effective. The resultant community should be a community of learners who are open to the possibilities, but are also willing to succeed at times and to falter at others. Quick success is not enough, because then the participants go home and shut their doors to the dialogue. Instead, the work must never be finished, and, although players may change, new people must be engaged in the process of community building if progress is to be long lasting and continuing. It is not the immediate solution frozen in time that this offers schools. It offers instead a way to continue to incorporate the new with the old and come into the next century with possibilities.

Making the Ideal a Reality

The coming together of representatives from the two organizations to work toward the joint undertaking of designing and eventually building and operating a public school on the university campus was interpreted from the perspective of the semiotics, or life signs, of the new society formed during negotiations. The interpretation of these signs gives them meaning, and this was done in order to generalize those conditions that lead toward collaborative, community problem solving. This cannot be accomplished in isolation from the social cultural dimension in which events exist, therefore interpretation (hermeneutics) is not only of the texts and artifacts produced during the three years of negotiations, but of the motivations and obstacles along the way, which are related to issues of control, politics, and power. These are socially constructed variables that depend on analytical interpretation to describe and give meaning to the social world.

When looking at textual artifacts in this study of minutes, notes, agreements, and other written forms of communication, analysis can't assume that the meaning is produced as the author intended. In fact, each and every formal and informal communication was subject to intense scrutiny by all participants for evidence of control and power of one of the organizations over the other. The organizations were protecting themselves by scrutinizing and assigning motivation to each other. The endless delays in the lease agreement are a good example, with lawyer talking to lawyer over one word here, another implication there, each trying to protect their respective organization without regard for the collaboration, which was extremely frustrated by this process. It is this struggle for meaning and for the uncertain outcomes that is studied here. This is like the rewriting of the now popular classic *Little Women,* which dumbs down the Victorian text to a series of events for widespread reading by a public used to television. The new text loses the very quality that made it an enduring classic, that of providing meaning to the reader. This is seen even more clearly by viewers of the movie in which personal interpretation by the writer of the screenplay, the director, and the actor were removed from the viewer as they directed attention to their meaning. Much of the interpretation was similarly preestablished for participants in this project by the frame of reference of the parent organizations; there often was an atmosphere of predictability as meaning was derived from the agenda set well in advance. This happens when negotiation is replaced with announcement, and power and control are the hidden purpose.

Hodge and Kress (1988, 18) suggest that analysis be directed toward the culture, society, and politics of the system under investigation. This includes the verbal language used, how each person speaks—whether formally or informally—and the significant concrete practices represented by the language used. In addition, each of these is grounded in time, within the context of the history of the project, and the process of change as it affects each of the participants and each of the organizations. The method of meaning making throughout this process was my interpretation of the transactions that occurred within and between the systems of operation of the parent organizations and the persons who represented them. I interpreted the events, assigned purpose to them, and through the sifting of that information, tried to move the process toward collaboration.

To provide this understanding, I had to communicate to the reader the seemingly endless time each part of this process took. Not only did each parent group operate under a different timetable, but also the negotiations were speeded up or often slowed down because of some outside event or outside regulatory influence that had its own sense of time. Every moment in this process led to some previous time or event that influenced the present. All exchanges, all relationships, were influenced by previous history and had to be encoded when that history was not made public. Thus, my description, although I tried to be linear, sometimes moves back and forth through time as I constantly tried to interpret and search for the meaning behind the event or the exchange. Every relationship was subject to this transformation from the present to the past in order to create understanding. Every concrete event also had motivation derived from the real life led by participants from each organization's social reality. Often, the effect is not conscious to the participants; at other times it is overt. The influence on present practice, however, is real and must be understood to have an effect in moving the groups toward achievable goals (Hodge and Kress, 1988, 35).

Clues to these relationships and motivations are found in the physical artifacts of the exchanges. Hodge and Kress (1988, 52) suggested these artifacts include physical relationships such as where people sit at meetings, the distance between participants from each organization, whether participants sit together creating a united front, or whether there is intermixing among them. The power of distance keeps each side as a separate organizational structure and influences the way each side perceives the other. The formality or informality of the dialogue is also important. Each organization had a formal language and an informal language. When meeting with persons from another organization, especially if the intent is to collaborate, attending to whether the formal voice is used becomes an important clue to the purpose of the exchange. When the dialogue is informal, there is shared understanding of language; when it is formal, the language can be used to mystify, defer, wield power, or subvert the process. Task assignment, too, can be formal or informal, following the titular roles of the parent organization, or represented by everyone doing what has to be done to get the job done.

The Personalization of the Organization

This analysis of process dwells on theory building. To guard against presuppositions embedded in my own perceptual understanding of events, I tried to determine motivation as it was embedded in the context of people and relationships, housed in the theory of how each organization understands itself and circumscribes the way people function within it. People behave in ways determined by the logic of their own organization, which transmits messages about their identity, status, and power within the system. These messages, overt or covert, are translated into beliefs about what is possible and what is not possible through the roles played and the exchanges that take place outside the organization. Inside and outside formal organizational exchanges, people operate in ways that are consistent with the system they represent. This is a manifestation of belief. An example of a belief system that is not fully formed is found in the teacher's lounge, where faculty may complain about the operations of the structure. They resist the alignment of their belief with that of the organization, or they resist changes imposed by the organization on them while clinging to the old. Fully integrating the culture of the organization with one's beliefs means that the social reality of the organization is not only embraced, consciously and unconsciously, but also that there is congruence with the ideological content of the mode of operation of the organization.

Educational systems operate from paradigms, which determine the dominant modes of organizing and transmitting the culture of the organization. Colleges of education have low boundaries and weak boundary maintenance, making them hard for the outside world to understand and interpret. Individuation of knowledge through specialization implies that the learner lacks the power of the specialist. This outside world, beyond the university gates, or those who come to the university for knowledge, keeps distance between faculty and the community. The public school system, on the other hand, has clearly defined boundaries, which are maintained at all costs since they define who the system is and their operation is equivalent to who they are. The presence of elements of boundary maintenance, whether cohesive or not, is an element of power wielding and solidarity within the organization. Both organizations in this study, in their own ways, repeatedly invoked this wielding of power: the public school system in an orderly, somewhat more predictable way, and the university through apparent disorder and lack of cohesion, by the artifact of not being able to make up its mind. When the boundaries of each group became more transparent, they signified the moving closer together of the two groups. This transformational facility to permeate the boundaries of each organization is an indicator of freedom; it is the breaking down of constraints that permit the beginning of community building. But, this is not an easy process to negotiate. Each organization has to be willing to explore interactions that are not part of its cultural milieu, and operate in ways that are exploratory on both organizations' parts. This forward movement does not have a plan, and it gets its momentum from individual exchanges between people who begin to change their organizational beliefs about the other system.

Overcoming traditional kinship lines within each organization is also evidence of boundary breaking. Changing those lines is anticultural to the established climate of each organization, but particularly critical for the public school, which is dependent on top-down hierarchical structures. In traditional relationships, consistency of mission and understanding of the ways of operation within the organization are manifested in the normative understandings that are more important than innovative linkages and design. The conditions of the very life of the parent organization are threatened. The basic elements of the ready-to-wear school are not sustained. The structure—the diagram of the organizational scheme—is not upheld.

Enculturation or resistance, production or reproduction of meaning? What was the goal for this project? Which did we agree to work toward? The commitment to create new carries with it the need for the creation of a new structure of work. This is the reason for the formation of a separate sustainable structure apart from the structure of each parent organization. It guards against one organization's imposing its structure on the other. Although I believe that we approached this new structure, and that it will come alive, with the sustained commitment to and daily operation of the school, no autonomy of operation and legitimacy was given by either side in order for this to begin as yet.

Organizational Habitus

The transition to new forms of working together necessitates awareness of the role of culture in the reproduction of the social structures of each parent organization. In this project there are three such structures of which to be aware. The first is that of the university culture and the college of education; the second is that of the public school downtown administrative staff; the third is the school structure, which was yet to be clearly determined. It is of the latter that we can, nevertheless, make some predictions. The interaction of the first two during the planning and negotiating phases of this project was typified by each operating from its own perception of reality, which is the taken-for-granted part of the everyday life within any organization. The latter represents and is a glimpse of the organizational culture of that organization.

Bourdieu (1993) called this perspective habitus, and it accounts for the creative, active, and inventive capacities of people within an organizational structure. It is not that they operate from a universal mind (5) but that they follow principles, organizing practices, and representative understandings that are objectively adapted to their everyday dealings with the internal and external environment. Conscious adaptation and practice that keep people in line with the commonplace operating procedures of the organization do not really occur formally. Instead, there is an unconscious compliance toward the way behavior is supposed to be when you live and work within a prescribed environment and as you represent that environment in the way you act. This is not restrictive since there is a real process whereby newcomers to an organization learn to behave in ways that are congruent to the organizational goals. They come to establish beliefs about the organization and what is appropriate behavior within that organization wholeheartedly. The production and ultimate reproduction of these behaviors become the norms of operation.

Bourdieu (1993, 6) viewed the process of acquisition of these behavioral norms as the result of inculcation that is a long time in the making and starts within schools themselves. The agent of cultural reproduction—the determiner of taste, appropriate behavior, and the dispositions throughout life that are transposable to situations removed from the learning environment—is the result of the acculturation process. Everyone attends school. We understand the norms of behavior and the expectations of school. The overt teachings, and more importantly, the covert teachings, become internalized into our beliefs and dispositions, and they are tied to what appears to be effective practice. Why are schools so resistant to change? The very thing we are trying to reform is the structure that produced our dispositions and generated our practices in the first place. School is the structure and education is the social situation in which the habitus is formed. It creates the rules, regulations, and laws by which we function in society, and changes in that structure are often either superficial or resisted. Within the field itself there is competition, but it is competition for resources, position, and control (7).

An example of this is the class war between the College of Education and the school system. Each protects its own capital, the school system by supporting the ready-to-wear school, and the college by supporting innovation, research, and the production of knowledge, often in the form of critiques about the status quo. This capital is the secure knowledge from which each operates with surety that it is correct. In order to interface the one with the other, each must have the skills of habitus of the other; each must be able to get into the mind of the other or else each loses at the outset even before the start. For example, no knowledge, skills, or talent in understanding what the other participants have, and no perceived need to acquire that information is a big error on the part of any effort to collaborate and make changes. The expectation that one side will change because there are compelling reasons to change is naive. The expectation that one side will change because of the status of the other, say, of the university as expert, also will fail. These scenarios are not realistic. Each operates from the assurance of its own legitimacy; each views itself as equally valid, supported all along with its own worldview, its own habitus. The other organization's game is not this organization's game, and the rules of the game must be known to all before there is any show or pretense that the two sides are working together. In addition, each has symbolic sanctions and agents of legitimization of the learned societies through which it is given status, such as accrediting associations.

Through consecration, these associations co-opt the organization (Bourdieu, 1993, 121), and this results in only extremely slow rates of evolution since they function primarily as maintenance of a social system that functions for the reproduction of the structural culture, which makes school systems look like one another and colleges of education resemble each other. Sincerity is only achieved when there is harmony and alignment in the expectations of position (the work that each does), the dispositions of people who are participating, and the roles that these people play (Bourdieu, 1993, 95).

What happens when you enter the game with conflicting habitus? Bourdieu (1993, 8) suggested a transfer of concepts from one field to another that requires analogy building and metaphor and myth creating, so that one organization becomes understood by participants from the other organization. The effort, then, becomes one of placing each in the other's shoes, or at least attempting to do so. Although this sounds like a simple thing to do, it is very difficult, since it requires that awareness of the limitations of personal habitus be conscious. Renewal for the field necessitates this collective consciousness since the structures themselves are what stop innovation and reform. Without this understanding, critics on both sides view the same events and remarks to their own advantage, often at the expense of the other. They are totally convinced of their own point of view.

How can the transfer of the strategies and dispositions of one field to another be accomplished? Part of the process of this study identified at least one element of this transfer. The element of trust was the catalyst. This came about through the sharing of the fields and the recognition by the school system that at least one or more participants from the other side understood their habitus. The recognition that they were dealing with people whom they thought understood their position and beliefs in relationship to their field may have been based on the assumption that these people would support them and behave in ways counter to their own culture. Perhaps they thought they would convince their own culture to condescend to the power of the other's views. People with dispositions from the university organization who supported rather than criticized were welcomed. This became the battle of the "waiting-to-be-made" school with the "ready-made" school.

What is the catalyst for reform and change to that "waiting-to-be-made" opportunity? Is there a need, as Bourdieu suggested, for a creator? (1993, 76–77). What does not work is cynicism and criticism. What is equally nonproductive is public clamor for reform when what is really wanted is more of the same, only of higher standards or quality. Remember, the success, or apparent success, is always viewed with the eyes of the habitus, whether that habitus is of the public, the school system, the university professors, or the teachers on the front line of implementation. A circle of belief that is both myth and reality, like the Garden of Eden story, surrounds the ready-to-wear school. The failure of reform and the end of innovation are sacrilege to the norms of habitus. Crisis is imbued with the creation of the reform, as the source of failure is misdirected. This is typically the case in schools when the messenger is blamed for failure, not the source. While working at a school site I once walked into the administration office with a viable suggestion from all the exceptional education staff to speed up the testing process, which was way behind schedule. I assumed the other staff members were behind me, but when I turned around, I was alone in the principal's office. I was the deliverer of the message with no apparent support from anyone.

How is habitus penetrated so that there can become mutual understanding and working together toward common goals? Since habitus is a system of dispositions, there is a relationship between position and disposition. By this I mean that the first aspect to be understood and overcome is the titular roles people play in an organization. Then, the organization itself has a name and reputation larger than the life of the people who work within it. Repeated contact over time allows the outside world to imbue the organization with capital, real or not. This consecrates the name with symbols of success in the business and dealings in the everyday world. It also allows the commercialization of the organization, the ready-to-wear of the system, and the trading for prestige and authority within the moment. It stops the creation of new ideas, since the ready-made is acceptable as an expectation. Short-term gains are traded for long-term solutions and systemic progress since they require time, resources, and personal commitment to generate and sustain interest.

Inherent Impediments

As long as professors write for the uninitiated hoping to initiate them into the university habitus and school systems continue to function to methodically develop or create dispositions of the educated person with the motivation to perpetuate a habitual culture, the consecration of the existing social order will continue. There is fertile ground to create new culture, but the histories of both organizations and the resulting school culture keep the barbarians at the gate. Society must consciously attend to this. It must create environments where the pure gaze of the viewer is of Eisner's connoisseur—the person who makes up his mind rather than having it made up for him, who is conscious that decisions can be made and that there is a real possiblity of rejecting the ready-to-wear that has been made for him.

Schools can become the catalyst for the creation of new communities. These communities understand that situationally real people operate in ways consistent with the past. In other words, people cling to the old because the old is comforting or the old is an accepted part of the organizational history they have internalized. The new community works in different ways, endeavoring to improve that structure and allow for better opportunities for continuous learning and the creation of new linkages that broaden the realms of support. The new community has clients that participate and help shape the services they, the clients, need. Every school resulting from this is different, has different needs, and is not restricted by the habitus that stops the culture building from being site specific.

This school environment sustains change. The participants understand why they need to restructure and are willing to explore how to do it. They are clear in what they want for their students, what their unique and varying needs are, and that these students, and their families, are more diverse and unique than they are similar. Therefore, decisions concerning what is most important to know, how to transmit that knowledge, and how to provide the supportive climate within and around the school community that supports this is their work and the mission of the school.

To get there, the system of operation must change. There must be an open forum for the sharing of ideas. The breaking down of the boundaries that restrict this is the heart of what collaboration is all about. How to sustain and support the open forum rather than rely on the old habits of operation that impede progress becomes the focus for sustaining the collaborative interactions between all who have a stake in the school community. This school community and all the people who participate must share a vision for the life of the school. This vision is not carved in stone, but always is in process, like Dewey's perspective of the emergent democratic society that exists because of full participation in the daily life and on-going process of education. This vision has been corrupted and disrupted in the name of science, technology, and politics, and the result is the destruction of communities and the support they once offered to children and families.

There is also a syntax of how people avoid change. Their own inner voice directs them to listen and speak with the language of the norm of their organization. It is a model of communication learned so well that it becomes part of the unconscious and directs the inter-action that occurs between people within the same organization. These patterns establish the generalizations, the possibilities, and the behaviors and allow for selective attention when participating in joint meetings. As people from two different organizations meet to-gether, each of the participants listens with their own frame of refer-ence and reports with their own language. This causes the reality of collaboration to be distorted.

The creation of community must not be left to chance. It won't happen anymore by proximity of living, because of transience, im-migration, depersonalization, and technocracy of our daily life. We are more removed than ever from our neighbors. The stuff of estab-lishing community, with school as the focal point for community, is the ethical nature of interaction among the people who live there (what they want, need, and aspire to), what they value for their young who are the future, and whether they view schools as the opportu-nity to create that future through education. This community also cares for each other, something we have left long behind. They care for the children of neighbors, for the lowering of competitive atti-tudes that drive people from each other, and aspire to the moral dimension of caring about self as part of the larger community that they are integrated with. Each of the community-based projects, Sizer, Comer, Goodlad, and so forth, has built into it the under-standing that the establishment of a unique community is required in order to sustain the collaborative nature of each project. Once competition for status, resources, prestige, or power enters, there is a loss of community purpose. The failure, then, is of community, and it disregards individual students; but how many students and fami-lies do we risk losing by not trying?

In order to change, a new set of experiences to meet new challenges and allow work to occur in different ways must be established through the creation of a new syntax, a new frame of reference or point of view. This break with the past habitus is what collaborations are after. Forging new ways to seek collective outcomes and recognizing that there are many paths to achieve success are part of the process. Crucial, too, is the acknowledgment that success is measurable in many ways and should not to be restricted by the signs of success of one organization over another, by one set of beliefs and values over the other. This takes planning and a positive outlook of shared possibilities. It takes a language that is equally positive and supportive, that is based on cans rather than cannots, on possibilities and visions for the future.

Chapter Two
Introduction to the Process

In June of 1991, the College of Education (COE) of Florida International University and Dade County Public Schools (DCPS) entered into a long-range planning effort to design and eventually build and operate a public relief school on the university's main campus in Miami, Florida. The school site is on a five-acre plot of land on the northwest edge of the campus which lies on the northern path taken by Hurricane Andrew.

Long before Hurricane Andrew, the possibility of such a collaborative effort evolved through talks with previous superintendents of DCPS, the president of the university, administrators, the COE dean, and interested faculty members. Between the summers of 1991 and 1992, a small group of interested faculty members met with DCPS administrators in curriculum and instruction for ongoing talks about the possibility of a campus site for a public school.

The formal collaborative effort between DCPS and the COE and the mechanism for making the campus school a reality came about through another effort: the preparation of an America 2000 New American Schools proposal, which allowed participants to work together and get to know each other, while providing a mechanism for further joint efforts. Of course, DCPS participants were assigned to the task by superiors in the hierarchy of the organization, while COE participation was voluntary, except for the formal organizational leadership. Although the final proposal was not funded (we did make it to the last round of thirty, but were eliminated when lack of funding necessitated decreasing the number of awards), the process of joint meetings and exchange provided a process to go forth with the campus school project. By September 1992, a formal organizational meeting was held with four members from each organization, titled the Steering Committee, who hashed out the details of a proposal for a school on campus. These meetings continued formally and informally for the next eighteen months before a final proposal was ready to present to the school board and the university.

From the beginning it was clear that there was considerable distance between what each organization wanted from the collaboration. Negotiating the distance between the wants and realities of a compromise involved dimensions of control, power, and face-saving. The university wants, I believe, consisted of participation in an experiment of possibilities, reorganization, and philosophy, and in the opportunity to have a site for research and development accessible to COE faculty and students. For DCPS, wants included maintenance of a structural and curricular integrity characteristic of this very public school system, the acquisition of a school site that would serve an already overcrowded area student population, and the utilization of university facilities that would cut costs in construction and maintenance of the school.

Each set of organizational needs had to be balanced with the needs of the community. The students would be a majority minority, limited English-proficient population, and curriculum and instructional initiatives had to be appropriate and compatible. The concern of maintaining an achievement orientation also had to be balanced with an emphasis on innovation, experimentation, and research.

The result was a process of delineating and clarifying purpose internally and externally for each organization beginning with the first formal meeting of the Steering Committee. This group drafted the working principles that described the land, school size, principal selection, architect, administrative structure, budget, philosophy, plant, parking, and committee memberships. Each of these, and other issues, would be revisited later, but putting them on paper moved the informal discussion toward the reality of negotiation. A commitment to accomplish what was proposed knowing that we were exploring new ground was evident in the players. Thus, once the commitment was made public, both sides agreed to proceed with the project in good faith.

Methodology of Data Collection

What I have just described succinctly is the public record of the beginning of the process of negotiation and compromise for the collaborative effort. It does not, however, begin to describe the subtleties of the process. From the very beginning I kept notes of the meetings for my own purposes. I was a new faculty member in the COE, having made a career change from a neighboring school district to the university. My doctorate was in curriculum and instruction with an emphasis on instructional leadership and change strategies. I knew enough about the way school systems worked to recognize early on that the college of which I now was a part did not operate with a sensitivity to the way decisions are made and people operate within large urban diverse school systems. At the same time, the school system found the operations of the college just as mystifying. Why couldn't we simply mandate and select people and assign them to tasks? Why weren't our status and success dependent on our performance of such tasks? Why couldn't we just mandate changes the way they did? Who was in charge? Who has the title? Who defines the roles and responsibilities? Why does it take so long to accomplish tasks?

As the negotiations proceeded I found myself taking more extensive notes in the hopes that I would better understand DCPS and be able to predict their wants and needs. I wanted to translate them into the negotiation process. My goal was always successful negotiation through completion of a proposal that would be enacted into a campus public school. I could not foresee how involved I would get personally, nor did I anticipate the role I would play as the process unfolded. But, I did seek to take notes that would be useful in some way to the process. Since I had become a participant observer, I had to attend to words and actions as prime sources of data along with document analysis in an effort to develop a scientific understanding of the association occurring in the natural settings of meetings, both formal and informal (Lofland and Lofland, 1984). This structured, naturalistic observation allowed this future analysis to take on aspects of psychological, sociological, and anthropological interpretation about why the behaviors occurred (Seashore et al., 1983, 392). The observer, myself, became the instrument for data collection, and immersion in the micro- and macroactivities of the negotiations allowed for explanation of the content and context of the events.

Three distinct types of narrative were analyzed. First were chronological minutes of each meeting—the formal record of discussion and decision making. These were shared with participants from both organizations. Second were extensive field notes, which had been elaborated on immediately after each formal meeting. These notes included portraits of participants, reconstructed dialogue, descriptions of physical settings, accounts of events of informal meetings and telephone conversations, document collection and analysis, depictions of activities and individual behaviors, and observer behaviors (my own as a participant and how my behaviors and awareness may have influenced the process). These notes are the clues to analysis in this study. My record of impressions and feelings, scrutinized later for bias of interpretation, provides the data from which this analysis proceeds. Third were personal notes on the process, which were often emotional reflections and my personal experience, both positive and negative. These notes were reflective analyses on the methods, ethical dilemmas, conflicts, and clarifications of meaningful events as they unfolded and were described from my vantage point as participant observer trained to be sensitive to the change process.

These three types of notations, I found later, collectively formed the basis for analysis through metaphor, analogy, conceptual understanding, and interpretation that is characteristic of a social analysis of educational innovation. This qualitative emphasis of process, people, and the cultural environment within which they operate provided an ethnographic basis to the ongoing reformation of the perceptual reality in which I participated (Bogdan and Biklen, 1992).

Methodological analyses of my field notes, documents formal and informal, and reflections were then categorized and coded. Episodes were classified as to type or problem, jurisdiction (inside or outside primary group), conflict, source, complexity, and verifiability (Goodman and Conlin in Seashore et al., 1983, 353–367). The categories of interpretation were meaning, practice, episodes, encounters, roles, relationships, groups, organizations, social worlds, and lifestyles (Lofland and Lofland, 1984, 71–91).

Meaning is interpreted according to organizational culture. In this study, each organization has a different structure, which will be described in Chapter 3. Understanding of the structure enables pre-diction of behavior during the process and the assigning of cause and effect to consequences that may differ from intentions. Variation in behavior is based on causal inferences that align to the structure of the organization and the maintenance of system needs. For DCPS this is functionalism in action, and charting the possibilities of change becomes subservient to the maintenance of the organizational structure. Thus, meaning is derived from the norms, understandings, rules, typification, and worldview held by the organization. This ideologically driven perspective can also be viewed from a constructivist stance in which meaning is derived from individual members of the organization, who define and redefine for themselves their own interpretation and course of action. The latter is typical of the way university professors operate within their organizational structure. Each player, then, has a different worldview, and the organizational structure is more loosely defined yet supportive of this perspective.

The practices of an organization are the rituals, taboos, and tone of the actions typical within the organization, while episodes are dramatic events or encounters, internal or external, that impact the process being studied. Encounters represent the way people enact their roles when they participate in the artificial social system formed when meetings occur. An artificial system of relations results from the maintenance of a mutual focus over time. Over the course of the three years of full development and negotiation, a situational artifact occurred in the next category, that of roles. Traditionally, people have ascribed formal, titular roles that are articulated by behaviors within an organization. These roles may be analyzed by social and/or psychological type, but sometimes these roles may be affected by encounters that make them less predictable. This was evident in this case when participants from each organization connected to each other in subsidiary ways and formed relationships external and often personal beyond their ascribed function. This changed not only the dynamics of the group but also the expectations each had for the behavior of members from the other group. Tradition was less influential when authenticity of purpose and commitment to collaboration became paramount in the negotiations.

The group refers to the way people within an organization cope and adapt to a changing environment. It also refers to how they perceive the enactment of that organization's formal, articulated goals and mission. The social world of the organization controls its ability to be responsive to external influences through change and adaptation. The lifestyle that the social world creates is the binding cultural unit of the organization.

Methodology of Organizational Structure

Organizational study can be approached from different perspectives. The case study method of the history of the organization emerged in the late 1940s. This method looks at how organizations instill values beyond the stated rational goals that serve to promote and sustain the stability of the organization over time. Gummer (1990, 43) stated that organizations are designed for one purpose, to maintain their structure; as such, they can perform only a limited number of functions that fit in with that structure. These structurally rigid organizations, common to centralized bureaucratic organizations, are inhospitable to conducting professional work and are best at routine tasks that monitor and control.

Another approach looks at organizations as institutions that exist in a process of creative reality; the process by which organizations operate is rooted in conformity, which in turn is lodged in the taken-for-granted aspects of the daily life and actions of the participants. Actions, those observable behaviors that outsiders see of an organization as it "does its work," are the external phase of this process. The second phase is objectivation, or the interpretation of an action as having a separate entity from the people who perform it. Third is the internalization of actions by participants as accepted practice over time. Etzioni (1975) argued that bureaucracies foster allegiance to organizational behavior, and that, even for professionals trained otherwise, the expectations of behavior guide and alter any independently determined rules and norms of conduct. What appears by this analysis to be conformity and internalization is, if we follow this line of argument, really the abandonment of authentic behavior that is not in compliance with the norms of the bureaucratic structure.

A third perspective emerged during the 1970s and 1980s (Scott and Meyer, 1984). It involves looking at organizations as a class of elements and by describing each organization by the commonalities and variations of those elements, all paradigmatic in nature. Analysis concerns the rational myths, shared belief systems, cultural symbols, rules, and requirements to which organizations conform that support their legitimacy and character. Adherence to these elements by participants is viewed as behavior to be rewarded. This analysis when applied to the two organizations in this study showed them to be most divergent. The professionalism of the university is defined by the individual within a context of a loosely coupled system, an organization of anarchy. DCPS, on the other hand, is an organization of status represented by roles and responsibilities that the bureaucracy defines. Each has tacit and explicit negotiation postures that are forwarded by allegiance to the organization. Divergence from these allegiances has costs that are different for the individuals in each setting.

The most current type of analysis views each institution as a distinct social sphere. Rather then searching for common values, actions, or elements that describe each organization, this newer perspective allows the observer to view each organization as a unique entity with social, cultural, political, and structural aspects. Here the two organizations involved have very different and distinct social spheres, thus the analysis and understanding of the evolution of this project was undertaken with an attempt at hermeneutic understanding of how each moved toward the completion of the project. Individual behaviors of some participants from each organization evolved based on the life and work experience each brought to the table. Persons with similar backgrounds interacted in ways typical of people who speak the same language. Others never understood why some people talked or acted in ways different from themselves because they refused or did not allow interpretation from the perspective of the other person. For these players it became easier to point the finger and place blame rather than seek understanding.

The organization in this analysis is an abstraction (Gummer, 1990, 68–69), and it exists at three hierarchical levels: the institutional external level, the managerial level for administration and coordination, and the technical/product level, where production of goods and services are. As we go up the hierarchy in dealing with issues, the interactions become more political. This political persona is depicted in the organizational climate through the politics that, for example, gender and race play in career advancement and affirmative action in the public school system, or the tenure process and personnel selection play in the university. Power here is politics along with manipulation, dependence, reward, and coercion, whether legitimate or otherwise. As described in Chapter 1, building community is difficult when power and politics are wielded as the controlling forces.

Of course, the analysis in this last dimension takes into account aspects of the three before. When we talk about the social sphere of an organization, we cannot help but talk about aspects of its history, structure, people, roles, and relationships that sustain it over time. The focus is whether the two organizations have spheres of practice that overlap, as in a Venn diagram, to produce the possibility of a true, long-lasting collaboration. The areas that cross both circles are fragile at best. They represent fleeting moments in which one organization may need the other for special purposes. When the need is resolved, the circles move apart again. The quest is to change the direction of the movement so that the overlapping areas become part of the operations of each parent organization and can be sustained over time.

Human actions are critically dependent on the perception we have of the world. Rational attempts to describe actions of people and groups fail to fully explain processes because those very processes are constantly evolving. Individual perspectives have multiple realities depending on which aspects of the process we are examining.

Postmodernism recognizes that a complete description of an event must take into consideration the separate worldviews of the participants. Interconnections can be accidental unless a partnership in a cooperative stance is fostered through an understanding and acceptance of the validity of separate modes of operation, understandings, and values held by participants from each group. Judgments of purpose by each side are valid interpretations based on local norms of group membership. Any changes that occur are projections of each group's worldview of the future, and, although the future is not predetermined, it is an opportunity of possibilities framed by the context of the group itself. These are not judgments based on good and bad, or right and wrong, but reflections of an appreciation for the institutions themselves and the people who work in them (Srivastra and Cooperrider, 1990, 1–12).

When we look at a cooperative effort and the establishment of a community of cooperation, we may make the false assumption that a totally new structure replaces the former structures at the expense of each organization. This certainly is not so and probably is the cause of failure of long-term systemic change. The "tragedy of the commons" of failed communities is that this merged structure, even when it is a temporary cardboard house, has no common understanding of each side's language, mores, and modes of operation. What Srivastra and Cooperrider (1990, 16–20) posited is that we renew our approach and create "transorganizational systems"—hybrid organizations that share information, solve problems, and are egalitarian in operation. They are nonhierarchical and have a synergy of their own as a result. These systems, then, can share the possibility of a collaboration because the participants are unbound, even if temporarily, by their own organizational ties, which present limitations to functioning as an equally shared community. These new systems also must recognize a shared fate and build new experiences based on trust, even if that trust does not extend beyond participants. Although the consensus established by a transitory supportive environment is fragile, it can form the structure of cooperative shared governance necessary for a project such as this.

This outlook, which emphasizes the collective good of the organization, generates the potential for a new social system of ongoing social reconstruction of reality. Growth-promoting relationships and the affirmation of worth and value of others are established through interaction and dialogue. Action is dependent on the dialogue of trust, and decision making is directed by the relationships established by participants and the positive outlook they have about the life of the system in which they are participating. This social construction of reality is actually a virtual reality, one related to each of the organizational cultures but with a new, shared positive imagery and a capacity for shared perceptions of a future of possibilities. People who participate in this virtual reality operate with a renewed value attached to their ideas which is detached from the value they have as objects with a role to play within an organizational system. Like Blake and Mouton's Cockpit Grid (Blake, Mouton, and

McCanse, 1989, 9) this collaboration has high people commitment and high performance outcomes because participants are committed to a common purpose based on a relationship of trust and respect.

The warning toward this optimistic stance is, as Bolman and Deal (1991) stated, a cynical, pessimistic frame of mind, which could influence how participants operate in this system. The result could be an understating and undermining of the collaboration when it is viewed as the wielding of power, as empowering through force of ideas and influence, or as coercion. Then the collaboration becomes one of control of agendas, control of meaning, control of symbols, and personal advancement tied to organizational status.

Organizational Culture as Unit of Analysis

The understandings we have and the elements that describe culture influence our beliefs about how organizations operate. Malinowski's (1944, 36) traditional, functionalist theory of culture derives from an anthropological perspective. The definition of culture thus derived is, "the integral whole consisting of implements and consumers' goods, of constitutional charters for the various social groupings, of human ideas and crafts, beliefs and customs . . . partly material, partly human and partly spiritual, by which man is able to cope with the concrete specific problems that face him." This traditional view is, like Rousseau's social contract, an effort to explain how people behave by identifying the general principles that bind them together and integrate them into permanent groups (55). This analysis also identifies the formal rules and roles in a cultural unit. The principles include reproduction of the organization through the formal bonds that sustain the structure; propinquity and continuity of exchanges, agreements, and cooperation; human physiology, anatomy, and the conditions of pathology of the participants; associations and voluntary groupings by individuals for initiatives; occupational ability, training, and preferences that differentiate workers; rank and status assignments, which create caste-like, status-laden conditions within the organization; authority origination, decision making, dispute settling, and enforcement of rules; comprehensive, or power-coercive, authoritarian control (Malinowski, 1944, 55–61).

This functionalist view differs considerably from the organizational culture perspective, which focuses on the textural elements of the events that collectively make up the whole of an organization's operations rather than on the organization itself as the precipitating factor in these events. Schwab's (Bell, 1993, 135) commonplace elements of curriculum analysis are a good way to explain this difference in perspective. Schwab identified ways to look at and explain events and interactions of people within contextual environments. First is the individual whose behavior is situational and must be explained based on the event while refraining from generalizing to other situations. This differentiation allows for a dialectical relationship between subjectivity and objectivity of the agent describing the situation (i.e., the participant observer in this study). Second is the event itself—the situation in the environment of the society coming together to accomplish a task. Third is the text, which is perhaps the most revealing way to talk about the culture of an event. Text refers to the language, both oral and written, used for reflection about an event, and the meaning or inference ascribed to that text. It is recognized that the user of the text is affected by exposure to it, and that interpretation is bound to the conditions under which the text is created. The community, then, is the pattern of interactions that emerge from analysis of the textural elements and the conditions of creation; the user of the text is the creator of the community, and each interpretation is valid because each creates its own tradition. My interpretation of the textual elements of this study probably is different from those of other members of the process. Each interpretation is valid in its own right, because the process I experienced— the interactions I had—are unique to me, and the meaning I assign to the process is my interpretation of the commonplace created by participation in the cultural organization.

Schein's (in Sackmann, 1991, 22) definition of organizational culture is, "a pattern of basic assumptions that a given group has invented, discovered, or developed in learning to cope with its problems of external adaptation and internal integration, and that have worked well enough to be considered valid, and, therefore, to be taught to new members as the correct way to perceive, think, and feel in relation to those problems." Culture of an organization is cultivated in the workers and represents a holistic, cognitive tradition imbued with symbolism, history, and values, which provide a basis for action. The elements that characterize an organization's culture are the expressions and artifacts that portray the norms of operation. But, these behavioral expressions are interpreted as the ideas, beliefs, and values that collectively form standards for actions of the organized knowledge of the organization (Sackmann, 1991, 18–21).

Chaffee and Tierney (1988, 5–6) described the strands in the web of meaning of organizational culture as the symbols, decisions, and actions; the interpretation of history, time, and space in relation to leadership styles (which is very different for these two organizations); and the use of information as it relates to power and position. They also suggested that conflicts are reflections of organizational life and that contradictions reveal tensions within the organization. All change, then, is orchestrated within the context of the culture of the organization, and "the cultural paradigm views an organization as a social construction where participants constantly interpret and create organizational reality" (10).

Why then is organizational culture so hard to decipher? Because we assume that there is a shared, homogeneous, leader-centered, managerial organization that directs and sets these norms. But, in complex organizations and in those with a less traditional structure, these elements may be determined by a much less decipherable scheme. Some of these artifacts are only observable when they are challenged by outside forces, internal revolutions, or change initiatives, and then they may be exhibited as resistance to innovation. Ott (1989, 2–7) described internal, predetermined assumptions that guide the patterns of behavior within the organization. These assumptions may be residual from early leaders who first guided the organization and whose influence still pervades the societal culture as it exists today; or they may be the result of purposeful enculturation into the espoused theories of the organization (Argyris and Schon, 1974).

Therefore, analysis and prediction must rely on the present phenomenological reality of organizational operations as viewed by the public artifacts: the language of the organization as the shaper and controller of assumptions, thoughts, and beliefs; symbols, signs, and titles of authority as windows on the operation; artifacts, material and nonmaterial, including situational behavior and organizational charts that create, maintain, and share meanings and perceptions; patterns of behavior that are normative, ritualistic, or predictable; beliefs and values that ideologically justify behavior (Ott, 1989, 24–38). Ott (51) warned, however, that a dynamic interaction occurs when we analyze organizational culture and that it transcends the artifacts, which are mere pieces in a puzzle. Each piece, when viewed separately, does not give a clear picture of the whole and may subvert observers who tend to wallow in the microaspects at the expense of the whole. In the quest for the whole, it is the symbolic frame (Ott, 58) that gives direction; meaning and interpretation are more valuable than the reality of events, and ambiguity precludes rational problem solving and decision making.

The organization is symbolically constituted and sustained. Patterns of significance are interpreted by deconstructing the whole for meaning. We can interpret and decode by the symbolically constituted world; we can critique by interpreting the symbolic forms to give meaning to the life of the organization (Frost et al., 1985, 66). This will be accomplished by analyzing the artifacts (written products and communications) for meaning and by focusing on their symbolic importance; by analyzing dialectically to preclude linear, cause-and-effect interpretation (as in the predicting of behavior and responses of participants); by looking at bias in the language of the social order of the organization (was it the university language that dominated or the public school system language?); by using the psychodynamic dimension of motivation as a framework for understanding symbolic meaning (why do people act in the way that they do both formally and informally?); by viewing and creating metaphors to explain events; and by analyzing the purpose and political implications and interests served by the symbols (Frost et al., 1985, 66–67).

Frost et al. (1985, 326–328) described four organizational forms: rational culture, ideological/developmental culture, consensual culture, and hierarchical culture. Each has its own embedded theory of effectiveness that governs the rules of operation of the culture of the organization. The hierarchical culture internally is formal; provides continuity, stability, and control; and is formally evaluated through accountability measures and documentation. This centralized, integrated scheme is externally viewed as the rational culture in which individuals make decisions toward goal achievement, and performance is efficient and profit oriented, while maximization of output in the real-life market directs all operations. This closely resembles the operations of a public school. The consensual culture is clan-like, internally focusing on the development of human resources through discussion, consensus, and a cohesive climate that fosters morale-building and teamwork. This persona supports differentiation, decentralization, and flexibility, and is externally viewed as the developmental culture in which intuitive insight, invention, and innovation are possible. But, revitalization requires external support, finances, and growth-sustaining potential, or, as Frost calls it, adhocracy. This clearly is the modus operandi of the university, except that often the elements are frequently not present in order for the university to make the transition toward the external focus.

Organizational Culture:
The University and the Public School

It may be assumed that within a profession there are similarities of organizational culture. This is not true for the two organizations in this study; the school system and the college of education within the university have different missions and different assumptions. As a result, each works in its own way. The public school system is a unified whole politically, socially motivated, and legislatively constrained. The university is a loosely coupled group of individuals who view themselves as largely entrepreneurial and as removed and protected in their work from shifts of power and authority that are politically and socially motivated. This difference is a key point in understanding the process of educational reform and change efforts. Belief that participants in both organizations are socialized in the same way by their common profession does not hold up. Just as on the national front where debate rages over the meaning of professionalization of teaching, we cannot assume the professional culture in a school system has commonalities with the professional culture of academia. As Ott (1989, 101) stated, "Their members seek truths within the parameters of their school's perspective." Thus, they respond to events in congruence with the historical response of their own organization. (This historical pattern of response of the two organizations is an element that had to be overcome in order for collaboration to be successful. Often the history was based on events that had long passed, but the effects of which had become institutionalized. An example is when DCPS asked that certain Florida International University (FIU) people not participate in the team because of some past event that had irked someone, the details of which were long forgotten.) Schein (Ott, 1989, 85) theorized that this historical influence is measured by the extent to which each organization utilizes its historical responses when faced with dilemmas and conflicts. This may be much more predictable for DCPS than for FIU because of the organizational elements described next.

There are three types of organizational climates and subcultures (Ott, 1989, 46): (1) Enhancing climates, such as DCPS, have compatible normative subcultures, all fully cognizant of the organizational goals, structure, and expectations. (2) Orthogonal subcultures, such as FIU, accept basic assumptions but subcultures hold some assumptions that are unique to themselves. (3) Countercultures, the third type, can be an outgrowth of the orthogonal, where conflict and challenge become operational. These countercultures may be positive influences of creativity and innovation, or they may cause division and rebellion.

What is the organizational culture of the university setting? Because of its orthogonal structure and the myriad of subcultures, this becomes a difficult analysis. Bolman and Deal (1991, 80) described the university as a headless giant of loosely coupled independent departments or divisions; the organization drifts with little internal collaboration and utilizes crisis management when faced with having to make changes. Leadership resides in career professionals who move to administration, while power resides in money, tenure, and recruiting of staff (Lieberman, 1990, 13–14). Cohen and March (1986, 3) saw the university as organized by hierarchies of problematic goals, unclear technology, fluid participation, and vague or nonconsistent goals.

Elsewhere (Slater, 1994), I sought to describe views of the university and the impediments and solutions to the establishment of a shared organic community life that positively influences creativity, innovation, and successful collaboration by being one with the larger community. Before the university can collaborate with outside organizations, it must vision collaboration within the organization. This has been complicated by a history of conflicting missions about the purpose and goal of the university itself.

The university has been described as a village of priests with emphasis on teaching (Benne, 1990); as a town with one homogeneous unity of purpose in rigorous, specialized research and scholarship (Flexner, 1930); and as a purposeful entity with responsibility to "preserve the connection between knowledge and zest for life, by uniting the young and the old in the imaginative consideration of learning" (Whitehead, 1954, 93).

This confusion of goals and roles within the university setting makes it difficult for outside organizations to understand the university mode of operation as a rationalized system. If we assume that despite these impediments there is a gemeinschaft, or shared local community life and existence, the university is not an administrative unit but a social reality emerging from a social life that promotes organic growth. This biotic community is the culture of the university, and it is created by the people in the organization through the linking of common bonds (Konig, 1968). "Participants recognize the community as a social totality, a social system unto itself, and thus individuals have a social identity formed through social relationships and consciously imposed limitations" (Slater, 1994).

Benne (1990) argued that the university community has lost these community-building elements because of fragmentation and confusion of aim and image, the inappropriate social organization of university life and effort, and outside pressures that divert the organization's energies to inappropriate goals. Mandatory activities subvert purpose and close doors to collegiality and dialogue. Individuals work in relative isolation in highly specialized hierarchical strands. This discourages crossing of boundaries within the university itself. How then can we expect the university to collaborate with the larger outside community if behaviors that could foster this engagement are not part of the ritual practice within the organization itself?

Cohen and March (1986, 4) examined the normative understanding of decision making at the university and its meaning for intelligent action. They suggested a normative theory of attention to scarce resources and a new theory of management, not of control and coordination, but one in which rewards are redefined as a raison d'etre for new faculty to be involved in remaking and redefining practice. This results in a transformation of culture—one in which active participation is valued and the worth of the individual is not recognized—not just an expression of service, which is viewed as having less value than research and teaching. This would foster the interactions necessary for collective sharing within, before attempts are made to mirror this in the larger community.

When each individual is an autonomous decision maker and decisions are controlled by no one, anarchy may result (Cohen and March, 1986, 33–37). Participants are accepting as long as imposition is not tried and there are effective information systems open to all regarding the organization. This results, however, in ambiguities of leadership, purpose (goals vary and change), power (who has it, who wields it), experience (does the organization learn from the past or is it a learning organization), and definitions of success (is it promotion, organizational output, or some other criteria, or do the criteria even exist) (195).

Newmann (1993, 9) suggested that collaboration requires practice, and that participants should work cooperatively in teams to collaborate toward achieving collective goals. Then linkages between partnerships of the public school and the university can harness the diverse community resources necessary to succeed in achieving common visions of interorganizational collaboration and can overcome the political, legal, and economic factors that support organizational independence, rather than interdependence, which must be guided by a caring community.

This is in stark contrast to the public school system, which is largely a utilitarian, compliant, cultural structure (Etzioni, 1975). Bolman and Deal (1991, 80) described schools as a stagnant bureaucracy that is a predictable, placid environment for workers, while it is top heavy in reform and administration. This is a rational system, predictable in behavior, clear in goal and mission, and relatively stable in orientation. What then creates the conditions for collaboration between these two organizations? Does the effort require extensive changes and reorientation?

The recommendation for the university (Slater, 1994, 12) is to, "Change orientation, change habits of the heart, work out conflicts between career needs and community bonds, and make the physical environment more community friendly, foster endeavors that reinforce commitment to the commons (Etzioni, 1993). Create at the university an urban village that emulates neighborhoods of old and share decision making based upon the good of the collective rather than at odds with it. Then we will have created a collegial atmosphere of freedom that would have the most impact upon ourselves, our students, and the society we are a part of."

An explanation for how these two organizations came to collaborate (Srivastra and Cooperrider, 1990, 205–214) lies in the creation of a transorganizational alliance precipitated by a common purpose necessitating the sharing of resources, information, and expertise to deal with an uncertain environment. This created a functionalist social system that shifted emphasis from the internal culture of the organization to an inclusive decision-making culture embedded in the larger community. This collaboration had good reason to be created. An appreciation emerged for players in each side's organization, value was ascribed to the partnership, mutual adjustments occurred to the traditional organizational structure of each, and a venture partnership was created. This partnership retained ties to the executive functions of each parent organization. Politics, social criticisms of each other's worldview, and leadership styles and skills still executed by members constantly influenced the process. But, the larger social culture was created—albeit accidentally perhaps—and, I believe, functioned in an atmosphere of trust. New networks and linkages were formed, and some common ground emerged, as you will see in later descriptions in this text.

Throughout the process of the creation of this transorganizational collaborative group, various internal and external pressures actively influenced development of this subculture. Internally there were elements of team building, conflict, control, and rewards. Externally there were imposed constraints from the parent organizations and the environment, which included elements of time, resistance to change, and the power of organizational roles. These elements are depicted in Figure 1, which shows the flow of information, interpretation, and feedback influencing both the parent organizations and the transorganizational collaborative group. What makes the newer structure more responsive to the environment is that it has

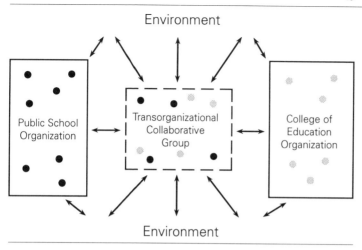

FIGURE 1   Flow of Information, Interpretation,
             and Feedback

multiple members who have different sensibilities and understandings based on their unique life and work experiences that can create
a synergy of response not available in the repertoire of the parent
organization. The environment, in turn, influences and is influenced
by each of the structures. The transorganizational collaborative,
though, has more ability to influence since it is multidimensional.
This will be elaborated on as the narrative of the collaboration unfolds.

Internal Pressures
Team building included events in which sources of reliance started
to move away from parent organizations toward internal support.
Conflict involved issues for which sources of difference and disagreement were resolved consensually. Control and attempts at domination through parent organization perspectives diminished over time.
Rewards for involvement for participants were less based in parent
organization approval and were directed toward a spirit of shared
collegiality of the group. Participants recognized that the newly
formed collaborative could have influence, reward, and success beyond the task of preparing a document "agreeable" to the parent
organizations.

External Pressures

Each organization understands and responds to time in different ways. For the university, time is relative, and process deadlines are less dependent on extensive links to other parts of the organization. For the school system, time represents finances, political feasibility, and approval giving, the last of which is critical to its mode of operation. These two perspectives were brought into an agreeable balance. Resistance to change emanates not only from the parent organization, but also from the individual who must alter his or her personal belief system in order to embrace the new. For the transorganizational group, belief in individuals who could be trusted was the major ingredient in overcoming resistance. Finally, power coercion of one perspective over the other is exhibited in the personal roles, task behavior, and projection of self exhibited by participants. This power-coercive atmosphere of operation was replaced through a reeducative environment in which people-to-people relationships and cooperation became more important.

Chapter Three
Constructivist Interpretation of the Collaboration

Collaboration between organizations does not proceed according to a prescribed set of rules, nor does it follow a timetable. It is, instead, a process that unfolds with a life of its own and proceeds through stages that may be unique to the endeavor. In a positivistic world, it would be possible to look for evidence of the finite set of conditions that verify the process from informal talk about working together toward true collaborative efforts. But, those of us who live and work in socially constructed worlds know that the quest for the provable set sequence is not finite. It is instead influenced by an infinite variety of unpredictable conditions that resemble more the chaos theory metaphor of the ripple effect of a pebble thrown into a pond of still water. Each event causes multiple contextual influences, and it is impossible to predict linearly cause and effect before the pebble is thrown. It is far easier to look at the effects and then to trace back to the source.

This chapter begins to construct meaning and interpret events by analyzing the effects of the process. We start almost at the end of the three-year process and look back and forth in time at how we created a final product acceptable to both organizations. This orientation provides a method for the constructive interpretation of why people and organizations posture and negotiate from their own perspective. Woven into the narrative is theory, practice, and research, both traditional and emergent, which serve as guides to sense making.

The End Is the Beginning

It is almost the middle of 1995, and the proposal has yet to go to the school board. The proposal is finished and has been tacitly accepted.

We are waiting for a formal meeting to package up our collective work in the format for official acceptance by the school board. The project has been fraught with delays of little consequence to its value, merit, and worth. The organizational administration of each parent organization is pleased with the process, and the delay becomes one of each side's not understanding real time in the other's operation. DCPS works on deadlines; everyone and everything has a procedure and a schedule. For them, we are not behind or in advance of their master schedule and building needs. For FIU, time is relative and does not play as important a role as the process itself, even if it is at the expense of completion of the task. The wait, then, is based on people's perception of the importance and relevance of the project in relation to their own agenda and to other projects that may or may not, in fact, be linked to this one.

The bureaucratic permission givers and legal decision makers on both sides have participated and continue to participate in the delay. They are playing a game that is removed from the people from both sides who worked on the project. Once these people are left out of the process, the organizational posturing takes over as each side scrambles for power and control. Indecision and inaction are pitted against a "do it now no matter what the consequences" philosophy or the legitimacy of the prior negotiations, and what is accepted and what is thrown away as consequences of delay or blame are largely inconsequential.

I came to realize during this extended waiting period that this project is unique as an opportunity for research on the conditions of success and replication of a true collaboration. The process of understanding has become more important to me than the documentation and analysis of the narrative. The text of the meetings and analysis has become secondary to the research base that emerged on the transorganizational system and how participants overcome the rules, roles, and responsibilities of the parent organization. My quest has become the semiotic understanding of the construction of this collaboration, and it has led to fields of sociology, philosophy, and theoretic organizational structure. Semiotics has provided an understanding of how meaning is constructed by allowing for the decoding of systems of symbols and signs in which each culture is embedded as evidence of meaning derived from surroundings. This knowledge reveals the tacit beliefs and ideals of each culture. It also provides the informational base to create a new way of operating and for individuals to enter an arena that may have become stagnant with old perceptions.

Collaboration requires that participants recognize these semiotic signs of the culture of the other organization. If what the transorganizational structure needs to function effectively is this understanding, then the interaction between people from each of the parent organizations should become more honest. That is exactly what happened here for some of the participants. They would behave in ways that communicated honestly "this is the way my organization thinks and this is why this or that idea for the proposal will not work." Instead of wasting time on that which was not negotiable, they allowed for movement in the process to occur because people told each other the truth. An example is the architectural considerations. There never was a time when this was a viable area to negotiate. The only restrictions were of land area, and much time was wasted in the beginning touring other facilities and talking about design innovations that, in reality, were state restricted and far above the allotted budget. Finally, informally at first, the communication that this was not a fruitful area to be spending time was shared.

Before I tell the story of how we came to agree, I must go back to describe further the elements of collaboration that I believe were created purposefully along the way. Collaborations exist at the end of a continuum of interorganizational arrangements, which can be described by complexity and sustainability over time. The most common type of relationship between a school system and a university is the network. This is characterized by professionals working in one school or many schools with teachers in order to enhance practice through expansion of the teacher knowledge or skill base. Sometimes this arrangement is just to experiment or explore possibilities for enlightenment. Clark (Sirotnik and Goodlad, 1988, vii) described networks as existing for the exchange of information and ideas. They are nonconfrontational (34). Networks bypass institutional formality; they are antiestablishment, not purposely designed collaboratives but partnerships between people. If the persons involved have no political power within their respective organizations, these networks produce no systemic change in the operation of each parent organization and do not exert meaningful influence on future attempts to form transorganizational alliances (Srivastra and Cooperrider, 1990).

Structured inquiry is a little more complex. Here, theory and practice come in contact with each other through noninstitutional participation of individuals working on a research project (one professional with teachers); helping in an evaluation project (paid or unpaid); designing and delivering an inservice workshop for the giving of information; or providing some other support from the university for an innovation that is requested and desired by the school system. Here again, there is no formal relationship that represents a shift for the parent organization, and there is no alliance established beyond that of the person-to-person contact that has become all too familiar and transitory.

Cohort partnerships are created for a specific purpose or task and when finished, the group dissolves. This partnership is external to each organization, as in grant and proposal writing and administration of funded projects, but when the project or funding is terminated, the connectivity of participants ends. It is rare for such partnerships to transform into institutional collaboration (Sirotnik and Goodlad, 1988, vii). The most desirable state is equal partners working together toward the solution of common problems. In a cohort partnership, a problem is identified and representatives from each organization come together merely to put into practice what is seen at the moment as a viable solution. The solution, then, becomes locked in time, a static resolution for an ever-changing field.

The conditions of partnerships are authenticity related to institutions, trust above the norms of the institution, recognition of self-interest, and anticipated identification with others (Soder, 1994). There is a politics of identity with others within each parent organization, and partners recognize the overlapping of self-interest in this arrangement.

Goodlad (Sirotnik and Goodlad, 1988, 12) noted that school–university collaborations have not been failures so much as they have been directed toward arrangements that have not been carefully created agreements and programs to which both the individuals and institutions separately and collectively have a sustained commitment. The problem becomes not one of creation but of maintenance on both sides so as to avoid a pathology of failure. Such efforts require planning, equality of purpose and parity, an agenda or device to bring together both sides because there is a need, and a structure to maintain momentum and connectivity (25–26).

Collaboration, as defined here and apparent in this study, is culture creating and constructivist; it creates, sustains, and maintains a long-term initiative whereby two organizations come together to create something new and in the process create a new form of sustainable collaboration that resembles less each parent organization than some new form. The creation is systemic. Success is characterized by knowledge of each other's culture and the planned overcoming of resistance by participants to working together that historically was the norm. The need to work together is driven by the knowledge that what can be accomplished is more than that which is produced separately, making the results synergistic.

Cooperation represents a low level of interorganizational work since each remains essentially an independent agency. Coordination is a middle ground between the two organizations, and often this is informal. But, collaboration requires interdependence between the agencies. What evidence, then, is necessary to prove that collaboration is occurring? Clues are found in the cultural linkages and established networks that go beyond the project. One is operationalized by management theory as structural, human resource, and political analysis (Bolman and Deal, 1991, 323). The other is symbolic and culture driven. Roles and norms are made and remade at the will of the persons; organization and reorganization of resources (people and things) occur as needed.

Clark (Sirotnik and Goodlad, 1988, 38) stated that the continuum from partnership, cooperative (agreement to work together), consortium to collaboration requires the development of shared responsibility and authority for basic policy-making to jointly plan, implement, and evaluate for improvement. The process must be egalitarian, have parity, and be dialectic. The results (Benne, 1990, 17) are pluralistic communities that exhibit bases of personal identity that are honored and processes of reconciliation available and institutionalized for use when conflicts arise. Bennis (Benne, 1990, 18) posited that resistance to establishing pluralistic communities is due to pyramidal structures and their mechanistic assignment of partial tasks to separate departments that remove the players from the entire process, which makes for inflexibility. Solutions to the limitations imposed by bureaucratic structures are projects that cause deliberate formation of other organizational forms that are democratic and characterized by cooperation. This produces novel resolution of conflicts that are more satisfactory to all parties than the perpetuation of the status quo. It also creates dialogues and new social relations as participants come to look at each other and construct new understandings—not understandings based on traditional expectations. Change in thinking is a social process that requires relearning on the part of the players (49). Benne wrote (1990, 65), "The greatest price persons pay lies perhaps in the suppression and denial of opportunities to develop themselves in directions that do not fit the specialized purposes of the association to which they have committed themselves . . . opportunity for development of self . . . do not occur naturally and may be actively discouraged . . . relations between competing associations . . . support development of mutually acceptable win–win resolutions to their conflicts."

Emergent leadership moves from traditional views of management to emergent collaborative stewardships characterized by process, interaction in relationships, responsiveness to the collective wishes of participants in the organization, pursuit of collective goals, allowance of bottom-up influence, and practice that is episodic (Ross, 1994). It is in the collaborative form that liberating opportunity for new direction can emerge.

The Formal Organizational Structures

Collaboration is an exchange of power, or at least a reforming of the way power and influence are negotiated and used. The organizational charts of these two organizations (Figure 2 and Figure 3) differ in formal structure, and this results in differing methods of operation and decision making.

The organizational chart for the university (Figure 2) is structured so that the colleges and schools lie a minimal distance away from the president. It is a horizontal structure with the lines of authority filtering through the faculty senate and provost. The College of Education follows the same structure, with the dean on a level playing field with the faculty assembly and administrative council, which advises. The associate deans form a second layer from which each of the six departments emanates. This structure makes for easy access to the dean, who can reorganize and restructure.

The DCPS organizational chart (Figure 3), in contrast, is a vast bureaucratic complexity. The multipage charts of each office and its management are further broken down into six regions with their own parallel structure of school operations. External to these are personnel management and services structures, personnel staffing, offices of instructional leadership, bureau of instructional support and curriculum development, and a bureau of special programs and exceptional student education.

Kierkegaard said that deciphering of knowledge takes an ethical imagination. This is a requirement when trying to understand how decision making occurs and what the lines of authority are within the school system. When trying to facilitate negotiations for something as complex as the design of a school, the external linkages required to complete the process between agencies require first that the persons who can make decisions be part of the process. This is complicated here by not directly involving the departments or people internally in DCPS who make the decision; often this is not the person who negotiates. Ultimately authority rests with the School Board with the consent of the union, parents, community, and those with external political influence. For this project, the decision to build a school on campus was made by a former superintendent and the president of the university. What was left to participants was how to negotiate the details of the project and then to make it a reality. This occurred as a process of establishing internal linkages between players in each organization who could gain organizational permission internally while agreements were negotiated externally.

The structure of the College of Education, although easy to understand and decipher, does not accomplish what the DCPS organizational structure does well. It is so loosely organized that the result is a lack of clarity of purpose and procedures to accomplish tasks. Feldman (Frost et al., 1991, 148–152) described the characteristics of such an ambiguity of intention and ill-defined preferences as one in which there is little agreement about what the organization should do, did in the past, or the value of present work. This is evident to observers as an ambiguity of understanding of competing ideas concerning what is appropriate for the organiza-

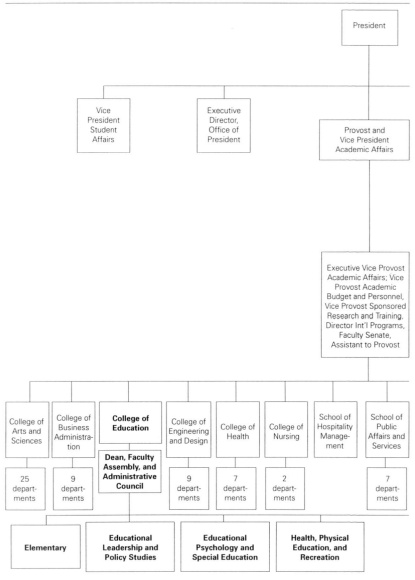

FIGURE 2   Organizational Chart—Modified
             Florida International University

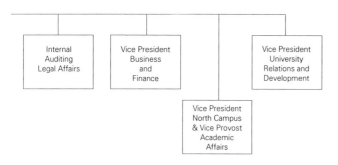

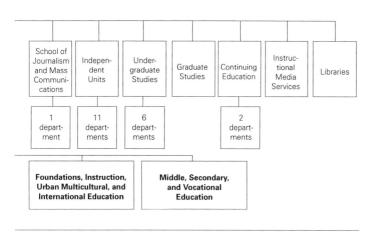

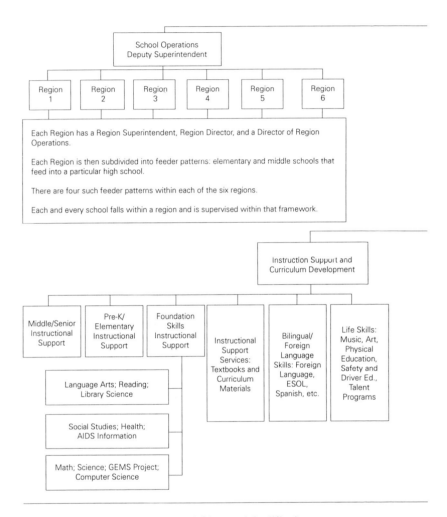

FIGURE 3   Organizational Chart—Modified
              Dade County Public Schools

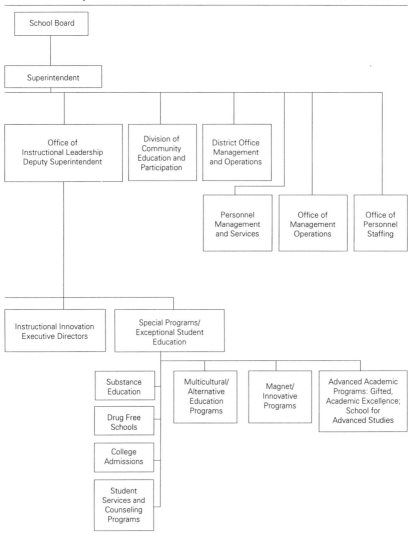

tion to do in response to calls of distress or liberation; ambiguity of history, the stories, and the perceptions people have of others, especially those external to the organization, is rampant. This was apparent in this project when people were chosen to be part of the Task Force, and DCPS requested that certain FIU people not participate based on stories of past interactions with them and perceptions of how the present process would be affected by these stories that had become myths. Meanwhile, FIU's choices were based on metaphors and myths of ambiguity of the other organization. These exist in a time warp of when their perceptions were established. Every time there is a new dean, the organizational chart of the college changes, players change, mission changes, and professors, who traditionally are independent, must reconstruct their understandings of what the purpose of the college is or resist and cling to old perceptions with the understanding that only the names have changed, but their work hasn't. University specialization and technicalization of education create an uncomfortable situation with humanists and moralists. Bureaucratization of intellectual life (Benne, 1990) is resisted and becomes the rallying call to maintain independence, so attempts to interact with other organizations, such as DCPS, become a blurred procedure based on false impressions.

The formal structure of each organization, discernable from the table of officers, departments, programs, and so forth, represents the social reality of the organization and the procedures that legitimize them. The myths of the formal structure are perpetuated by the profession, programs, and technologies. This rationalization gives rise to supporting structures like the laws of credentialing and certification representative of public opinion. Organizations use this legitimacy to secure support and survive. Their worth is measured by external criteria, such as accreditations for FIU and test scores for DCPS. The organization becomes isomorphic with the environment as it conforms to and is absorbed by the institutional environment. The continuum of organizational structure from productive organization of networks to confidence and stability of institutional rules is characteristic of large bureaucracies, such as DCPS. To respond to external demands, needs, and influences, the structure must be decoupled from the activities by making the goals ambiguous, by avoiding integration, delegating out of the organization to professionals, and making human relations important (Meyer and Rowan, in Powell and DiMaggio, 1991, 41–57). This is what we did in the evolution of new goals for the school.

This institutional isomorphism has sources that are coercive and politically legitimized (such as mandated school curriculum and laws), mimetic in response to uncertainty, and normative (such as the quest for professionalization). For DCPS, change is lessened through reliance on the organization, centrality of resources, uncertain relationship between means and ends, ambiguous goals, and reliance on academic credentials in choosing management and staff. This results in a homogeneity of DCPS professionals (DiMaggio and Powell, in Powell and DiMaggio, 1991, 67–76).

Scott and Meyer (Powell and DiMaggio, 1991, 124–129) noted that schools are weak technical environments and strong institutional environments. Administrative complexity at the school level is positively associated with the number of public programs participated in for middle and secondary schools. For elementary schools, the complexity of the district level buffers them from effects of environmental complexity. One area we sought to negotiate for the elementary school on campus was to eliminate or mediate this very complexity so as to increase the autonomy of decision making at the school site. The structure of area superintendent administering the school site principal creates a network of permission givers that could hamper innovation with the myriad of rules and regulations. We tried to increase the opportunity for innovation by eliminating or redirecting the routing of compliance and normative operations of institutionalism. What is lost, though, is the ability to do easy things that have a direct line of command and routine about them. The hard becomes easy to implement, but the easy to implement becomes a complicated task.

The organizational imprint is embedded when the structure is formed, and this defines the type of institution, teachers, and students of the formal structure and provides legitimacy. Certain aspects of this were not negotiated but accepted by consensus since they are little affected by organizational boundaries (such as student conduct, grades, materials). Other more formal agreements were worked out in a political arena of negotiations, such as contractual UTD (United Teachers of Dade) supported work rules. Since the carriers of the belief system extend to students and parents, other aspects of the process of coming to agreement had to be made in light of the culture of these external influences (Jepperson, in Powell and DiMaggio, 1991, 178). This process occurred while the push toward local control and standard-setting initiatives, such as America 2000 and Florida's Blueprint 2000, was being enacted, and DCPS created a competency-based curriculum for countywide implementation. In effect, whatever initiatives we wanted to implement had to be enacted within the context of these standards taken together to stimulate increased achievement of students.

Change Theory

Given the stability of the organizational structure of DCPS and the flexibility inherent in the COE, how did the structure of the negotiations between them proceed when the effort required changes in operation and participation? Change implies a new identity formed from elements of organizational culture, strategies, and leadership (Chaffee and Tierney, 1988, 28). Such changes are catalysts for chemical changes, not physical changes. To explain, *optical mixing* is the term artists use for the mixing of colors. Adding white creates a tint; adding black creates shades, which can be mixed together to create neutrals (i.e., shades of gray that are nondescript). Tints do not absorb, but sit on top of each other and can slide off and reveal what is underneath. Contrasted with optical mixing is the ideal of optical blending. Like Seurat's paintings, each point of paint retains its true characteristics, but the whole becomes the interrelatedness of each point of color and light, one to the other. The collective character is created by the blending accomplished by the perceiver. This is a useful metaphor for looking at and discussing the building of community and collaboration where the objective is optical blending, but what we get is the optical mixing of networks, cohorts, and partnerships.

Social collaboration makes its own narrative culture through internal communication and, in the process, questioning of the nature of the legitimacy of the decisions made in light of the name of the parent organization. In partnerships, cohorts, and networks, action occurs without assessing whether the solutions are appropriate to the problem and often the expectations of success do not coincide with the treatment. If you accept that the desired state is optical blending, solutions often are mere optical mixing. Therefore, when embarking on a change effort, planning is everything because if the course is nonlinear, the result is like a seedpod opening and sending seeds exploding all over. You never know where they will land, take root, and grow errantly.

Change is also imbued with contradictions and discrepancies. This fact is evident in this study. Curricular innovations or organizational innovations in education create imbalance, and adding or adapting just one element disrupts others, or the new may not be compatible with the old. This study required multiple changes on multiple fronts and, as such, required planned change to alter the pattern of decision making (Seashore et al., 1983, 177–180).

Bourdieu (1993, 4–6) described habitus as a feel for the game, a practical sense that directs and responds behaviorally to situations, though not prescribed. Habitus is the result of a long process of living in a particular place and acquiring the sensibility to act in ways that are appropriate and acceptable to that environment. This is a phenomenological response. The resulting dispositions are durable and transported to locations that participants operate in even if removed from the main site. All social formations elicit these behaviors and thus recreate the field that reproduces the culture of the organization. Change, then, requires that the field be reformed, and resistance to this causes conflict. The micro- and macrolevel social orders are loosely coupled; therefore, a long time is required to make changes in the larger social structure (Powell and DiMaggio, 1991, 295).

The theoretical perspective of micro and macroanalysis is attributed to Peter M. Blau (Calhoun, Meyer, and Scott, 1990). Blau posited a sociological structural interpretation of the interplay between internal forces within an organization's structure and the connecting, diverse substructures of everyday operation. For Blau, "Microsociology and macrosociology involve contrasting theoretical perspectives on social life . . . the units of analysis are different— individuals in the first case and populations in the second—and so are the concepts and variables—attributes of human beings in microsociology, emergent properties of population structures in macrosociology" (75).

	MICRO	
	over	**under**
over	Dynamic interaction/synergy Balance Congruence/validity mission Quality control Metaevaluation possible Feedback maximized Adjustments to data sources and effectiveness Trends/predictions Effects of implementation identified Focus on producers/consumers	No authority for adjustments No assurance data use Buy in not assured unless impetus outside Redundancy of product Drain resources Innovation in name only Lack authority on programs Feedback limited by uncoordinated data collection
under	Maverick planning No integration data between programs resulting in resistance to change Program improvement Responds to program needs in the narrowest sense Duplication of effort in programs Can't cause changes in other departments that may influence what this program seeks to accomplish Short-lived innovation Singular point of view Tension between departments, i.e., competing goals, competing resources	Lack leadership—or—leaders change due to lack of success, goallessness Confusion/chaos theory No data, no systematic support; only gut feelings/emotions Focus on individuals within organization, not on consumers Never have critical mass for adoption of new ideas At mercy of outside forces, usually mandated rather than participatory No growth, no data to corroborate efforts No improvement, accountability Confusion to clients; no quality assurance

MACRO (row label, left of table, spanning both **over** and **under** rows)

FIGURE 4   Micro/Macroplanning Dynamic Grid

Microanalysis is an individualistic and interpersonal representation of individual or subgroup behavior that is determined by social factors and interpersonal relations. Analysis of microstructures is a process analysis of small group, substructure, or individual behavior and decision making by members. Attention to microplanning alone results in isolated initiatives that have little long-term effect on the larger organization. These subgroups exist within an overall umbrella structure of the larger organization whose values and orientations comprise the macrostructural elements of any social network.

Macrosociological structures represent the paradigm of operations of the organization. They are the theoretical, ideological underpinnings of any operation. Macroplanning and decision making are visionary and provide overall direction for the organization, which then must carry out the vision by filling in the details of implementation. For Blau, macrostructures are the complex social structures of large groups characterized by complex distribution of social position along parameters of differentiation and interaction. Macroanalysis looks at phenomena that can only be understood by their abstract relationship to microbehavior. Blau's macro is a positivist, formalistic, structural analysis of the social life of an organization (Calhoun, Meyer, and Scott, 1990, 22).

It is important to maintain a balance between the macro and microstructure. Effective planning requires that a balance be established between the micro and macroelements so that effective, systematic feedback can be used to maintain the equilibrium in the organization (Slater and Gallagher, 1994). The matrix of consequences of depicting the consequences of too much or too little planning is depicted in Figure 4.

The least desirable planning cell is under micro/under macro. It results in a state of confusion for participants as the organization appears goalless and without clear direction. Change occurs by chance in a nondirected way, often making conditions worse than they were. Although neither of these two organizations plan in a way that would appear to be in this cell of the grid, there are times within the school system when the teachers would not understand, or not have an explanation, as to why they were required to implement certain initiatives and it might appear to them that planning was not a coordinated purposeful effort. The under micro/over macro cell can be equally disorienting as the leadership suggests vision after vision, directive after directive, and the people who work within the organization are constantly asked to adapt to new ideas and trends. This causes lack of stability and continuity, and the organization finds it hard to put ideas into practice. Often the university is represented by the behaviors and responses in this cell because there are always initiatives that are largely global that may be, because of the nature of the independence of the professors and programs, largely ignored.

The over micro/under macro cell results in lack of integration of each part of the organization with the other. Solutions to common problems cannot be dealt with holistically, and each subgroup duplicates the problem solving of the other subgroups since there is no vehicle to share solutions. Resistance to change results as each subgroup responds only to its own needs with often short-lived innovations. This is representative of both the university and the school system since individual schools make decisions that affect only themselves and each program or strand within the college certainly is independent.

The over macro/over micro cell creates a synergistic balance between the administrative structure and the parts of the organization in a way that maximizes effectiveness of the overall mission. It allows for innovation top-down and bottom-up and represents the ideal state of effective planning and evaluation. But, this frenetic activity must be balanced by moving from this cell into the under micro or under macro dimensions in order to be responsive to whether innovations work or whether new ideas and projects need to be instituted.

Powell and DiMaggio (1991) noted that new institutions establish the criteria from which participants discover preferences of action, but the costs are cognitive since participation is a phenomenological process (8–11). Macroinfluences create contextual effects (Meyer, in Powell and DiMaggio, 1991, 11) as new environments create a lens for actors to view the world. Transorganizations, like the one in this study, can become institutionalized when infused with value. These created institutions are macrolevel abstractions that are rationalized and impersonal prescriptions and have shared typifications independent of parent organizations and moral allegiance. The true collaboration is one in which cognitivism is paramount, and conversations, trust, and willingness to interact and recreate what are normal operations for each parent organization occur.

Bolman and Deal (1992, 4–5) described the cognitive characteristics of leadership for effective practice. "People define circumstances so they know what to do and how to understand what others are doing." They interpret each situation they enter by responding from one of the following organizational frames: structural, human resource, political, and symbolic (Bolman and Deal, 1991, 323). It is the symbolic that corresponds to the cultural construction of collaborations. The other frames provide processes to understand the procedures of the work of organizations and the influences upon that work, but the symbolic frame is the arena for the creation of new modes of operation. Higher education uses all four modes of operation, but school administrators primarily use symbolic and political interpretations. As Bolman and Deal (1992, 11–12) stated, the crisis of education is symbolic, one where individual and group reflection between peers can generate strategies, activate inert knowledge, and form new schema.

How are these cognitive constructs altered so that they reflect changes in belief, value, and action that approach the symbolic frame of Bolman and Deal? Benne (1990, 140–151) pointed out that the reeducative strategy of Lewin is the means to provide this change. Strategies for changing human systems (Chin and Benne, in Bennis, Benne, and Chin, 1989, 22–45) can be categorized as empirical–rational, normative reeducative, or power-coercive. The classical, liberal empirical–rational strategies try to enlighten the participants through the application of researchable proof that there is a more desirable and appropriate alternative. Normative reeducation strategies view man as a social product and assert that transactional participation produces reeducation. Change agents who consciously work out interventions that create changes in systems are the precipitators of these long-lasting, sustainable changes. The third approach, power-coercive strategies, involve sanctions, both political and economic. The withholding and convocation of status through position, laws, and manipulation of lines of authority create changes that we may liken to the optical mixing described earlier. From the public record, it looks like the changes are occurring, but when examined closely they are not infused into the beliefs and values of the organization.

Benne (1990, 140–151) suggested that the reeducation strategy be used to create cultural changes that are personal changes in people. To do this, he visioned changes of self and situations, the linking of social perceptions to self-perceptions, alternative conceptualizations of the same event, changes in the process of resocialization and reenculturation, value and belief changes that are systemic, and reconstruction through collaboration in group settings. Therefore, when DCPS says no to the demands of any institution, they are reducing their alienation from their own institutional organization and power base. The relationship between collective and communal is precarious, therefore bureaucratic organizations limit interpersonal exchanges in order to protect themselves. Collaboration, to be true and effective, must eliminate status if the formation of a community is desired.

Of the university, Benne implied (1990, 199), "Those who limit the work of reason to fact finding, or to social engineering conceived as manipulative salesmanship, will naturally conclude that the ideals that motivate people are inherently irrational in their content—'social myths' that move the masses but are quite beyond the limits of rational substantiation or disproof." Thus, Benne (1990, 200) stated that we must reduce our fear of differences, accept change rather than stability as normal expectation, expand trust of others, and clarify the nature of consent and consensus.

Seashore et al. (1983, 178) noted that planned change alters the pattern of decision making by influencing members of the different status groups into positions that are different from those of the policymakers. What is success for this project? For myself and the organization I represent, the process is the change effort, and if I have been successful in facilitating the process, and, in the course of analysis, can document changes in beliefs and attitudes, then we have created a true collaboration effort. We started this process clearly as two distinct, parallel organizations working in our own backyards with a tall fence separating neighbors. If the process were to be successful and collaboration to become a reality, then participants would continue to interact with each other in ways that are sensitive to each other and open and honest in the process. This can be both formal or informal, such as calling on each other for advice, information, or future work on other projects. There is evidence that this is the case as representatives on the subgroups from subject-specialized areas are, in many cases, working on other committees or projects with each other.

Chapter Four
Leaving the Past Behind

It is less likely that an organization will change its mode of operation than that it will continue on the path it is presently on. Much has been written in the popular literature about visionary leadership that endows the worker with changes in behavior that are consistent with waves of reform that will lead a company to future profits. Client service tied to quality of performance is imbued with the reward structure of businesses that are competitive and hopefully successful. Many of the metaphors of leadership are based on the successful models of management that have led to immense profitability of business ventures in other countries, especially the model of the Japanese. Consider the cultural beliefs of workers in this country. The cohesiveness of sublimation of the individual to the group, which supports unity of operation, is lost when applied to the individuality of the worker in the United States.

With the restrictions of bureaucratic life, it is unlikely that leadership metaphors of collective direction of resources and goal-directed behaviors of workers can be applied directly. Of course, there are instances in business in which such a transformation has occurred, such as the case of Motorola and the leadership of George Fisher, who led the company to envision the future, achieve the vision, and surpass it. No company in the cellular phone business is able to catch up. Inevitably, we study the Japanese and apply their techniques of operation while they study our successful companies. But, such a radical and uniform transformation in the world of public schools and public universities seems less likely. For them, change really is the overcoming of history and culture, which are well established and accepted. Change means recreating the very culture, myths, stories, and beliefs that are embedded in the daily accepted operation of the organization. That is the most difficult part of any change effort and is complicated further when the effort involves two organizations from two different worlds.

One comprehensive view of leadership is provided by Burns's (1978) transactional leadership, which involves exchanges. Participants want something from the leadership of an organization, such as better work assignments, pay incentives, status, or voice. The majority of relationships between workers and the decision makers at the top of an organization occur as a result of transactional relationships, and bureaucratic structures support this form of interaction.

Transformative leadership identifies an existing need among the followers and may exploit that need to engage each person fully in a direction different from that of the past. Motivation of followers is recognized as the mechanism to engage them in changing past patterns of behavior, but the followers also must believe in the merit of the change and feel that personally they participate fully in the restructuring of their beliefs about the effort. The leader, then, becomes a moral agent who converts followers into a new frame of mind, which creates a behavioral commitment to operate in ways different from before. Of course, few leaders in history have engaged followers in this way, and the reality of organizational life rarely allows such a redirection of belief or reallocation of resources to produce such changes. These changes are tantamount to little revolutions, and most organizations, as described in Chapter 3, rarely allow the opportunity and flexibility to affect the structure itself.

If this is the case, we then can propose that transactional changes can be forward moving for organizations, especially for collaborations that are transorganizational. Leadership, here, creates the macrovision for reform, but the task of implementation and making the microdecisions for action result from negotiating the reward structure of each. There is an opportunity for true collaboration to look transformative in product, but the real work is that of quality transactions whereby clusters of activity of product are central rather than the traditional transactions of position and role. When these behaviors are institutionalized, which can only be determined over time for the two parent organizations in this study, then the new becomes quality transactional leadership. Rewards for good transactional leadership require honesty in negotiations. These correspond to interactions in true collaborations if both sides understand and negotiate in good faith.

Change must be planned for transactional leadership to be successful. A carefully developed strategy results in changes in people and organizations, but must be designed around the diagnosis of a specific set of problems. In this study, the problems are both historical and normative, and only the introduction of a new set of players and leaders wanting the project to succeed (by consensual rational decision making) allowed for the microdetails of the interaction to proceed. Agents of change—persons or a person who intentionally take the necessary steps to orchestrate the effort—operate within social groups. These changes are people changes. Changes are in the construction and interpretation of events that are intentional. The result, when the transactional leadership provides the macrostructure to work out the microdetails of the exchange, is a synergistic resolution of the group effort that brings about something new—a true collaboration.

Kanter et al. (1992, 14–15) described change as being precipitated by external and internal forces that set things in motion. The interconnectedness produces movement that exists as one of three kinds. First, environmental movement is macroevolutionary, is related to wholes, and has the ability to endure over time since these movements are historical. Second, life-cycle movements are microevolutionary, where the parts of an organization move forward in relationship to one another in the daily internal operations of the organization; these movements are developmental and allow for the coordination of issues. Third, political movements create revolutionary activity and are characterized by power struggles, issues of control among stakeholders, and coercive benefits in decision making.

Applied to change efforts, Kanter et al. (1992, 15) noted that changes in environmental moves relate to identity issues that are macro. The relationship between the organization and the environment, between the assets of the place and the customer or recipient of service provides direction for the change. The maintenance of the relationship to those who confer legitimacy upon the organization results often in the maintenance of stability and changes serve to maintain and perpetuate the relationship in a changing environment. Because decision making here is dependent on external factors, the microchanges themselves do not produce reform since it is very difficult to reformulate the environment.

Microlevel changes of life-cycle movement are ones of coordination of the internal parts of the organization, which shape and structure it as the organization grows. These changes are apparent in the drawing and redrawing of the DCPS organizational chart when different superintendents are hired. Meanwhile, the organizational chart of the university remains stable, even if leadership changes. Changes occur only at the departmental level, which is artificially created to begin with. Professors continue their work with very little change even when placed in different departments. This type of microchange is not necessarily planned change as described by Burns (1978).

The political movement change takes the form of control, domination, and governance. These changes are ones that make over the structure of an organization and result from revolutionary takeovers, buy-outs, and power struggles. These changes rarely occur in the public sector.

Kanter et al. (1992, 16–17) described change as a process that is different for each of the three types of movements. Environmental precipitation creates processes that are macro in that they require change strategists to facilitate the process; the change agent is not necessarily the top leadership. Micro life-cycle changes are often in the hands of middle-level persons who are part of the process itself. They implement the change effort and often take the role or title of project manager. The idea for the effort need not come from them, but they have greater ability to implement successfully, especially if they are also strategists. Knowing what is wanted is less critical than knowing how to get there. Political processes disenfranchise those who are affected but do not have a say in the design of the effort. This results in tension and often in sublimation of the process itself. This is not an effective means to create change since it is allied to the power-coercive strategies that increase resistance discussed in Chapter 3.

The understanding of change as a process that evolves with leadership that respects the reward structure of each organization directs the narrative of this collaboration. It starts before the formal negotiation began and ends with the creation of the transorganizational collective that not only allowed the project to become a reality but also established a new mode of interaction between the two organizations. The narrative describes this process from the time of presteering committee, steering committee preliminaries, task force development, subcommittee negotiations, overlaid with elements that resolved in team building.

Historically, the narrative begins in 1991. Precommittee work on the idea of a campus school was transformed during this time into the writing of the New American Schools grant-writing project during which participants came to know each other while working on a cohort partnership project. As described in Chapter 3, this type of partnership rarely transforms into institutional collaboration, but here, the product of a campus-site elementary school was determined prior to the grant-writing process; therefore, the process turned into a trial run in collaboration and the success, not of funding but of negotiation and collaboration of ideas, provided the groundwork for advancing with the original project.

By 1992 preliminary meetings together to advance the school project, even without external funding, clearly looked more than ever like an evolutionary project for participants. I began to keep a daily formal narrative at this time. The artifacts (meeting summaries and notices) make up the bulk of the narrative before September.

The year 1993 was the phase of committee work, and by summer the formal buy-in phase was completed with participation from community and political interests. This continued through 1994, which became the year of waiting. The time lag, though, provided for real building of collaborative linkages, which led me to believe that the transformation from possibility to real transorganizational collaboration had occurred.

Precommittee Work

During the summer of 1991, I was asked by the dean to meet him at the administrative office of DCPS to talk about the creation of a school on campus. Preliminary discussion between the present superintendent and the president of the university already had occurred with the possibility of the elementary school becoming an integral part of the college's teacher preparation, research, and service mis-

sion. This had been an idea talked about by a previous superintendent and the university president. Why it resurfaced at this time is
not known, but clearly the initiative to begin real deliberation was
made by players not at this meeting. I thought there would be more
people there. As it turned out, the meeting was with a DCPS administrator who was soon to leave the school system, take a job as
superintendent elsewhere, and by 1994 return to the area as superintendent of a neighboring school district.

My notes from this meeting indicate areas of concern for all
future interactions. They document the areas of consensual differences and sources of disagreement or conflict issues, attempts at
domination and control by one organization over the other, what
were the rewards for involvement on the part of FIU faculty whose
primary focus is research, and how to keep the information flow
open so that any conflict-ridden dilemmas could be resolved. These
concerns did not change and were not fully resolved at any time
during the following three years, and I expect that once the school is
built and operational, they will continue to be areas of contention.
It will be the task of the administration and the university contact
person to be aware of and meliorate these continuing areas of concern.

The question of partnership from the perspective of the university initially focused on what it was that the COE wanted as a result
of this effort. Clearly an opportunity for advancement in teacher
preparation for the urban, multicultural, majority/minority Dade
County was an important goal. Faculty would have a setting to experiment, research, and explore innovative practices and evaluation
and alternative assessment techniques.

The laboratory-like setting we envisioned would provide extensive preservice opportunities for our students and an arena for experimental practice for teaching and learning. Envisioned was a continuum of services from licensed, in-field graduates who could avail
themselves of advanced degrees and in-service instruction, beginning teachers, preservice students, university students who are still
undecided as to their major and might be recruited, and high school
students who show an interest in teaching.

The meeting, dominated by the DCPS administrator, provided
us with the information on what we had to do to make the school a

reality. It was less an exchange than a process for implementation played according to their rules. If this school was to be a real partnership, then we had to define what the parameters were for us, what our agenda represented, what kind of involvement we wanted and needed, and how best to accomplish that. At this point, only the DCPS perspective had that clarity. The reasons for this lack of focus on the part of the university were that each person was operating from their own agenda, their own concerns and specialization, and their own past history of interactions with the outside. This is typical of a loosely coupled system. The other organization was structured to provide the clarity that permits players to enter relationships with other organizations knowing exactly what their organization wants and the parameters it operates under. The union, along with the president and superintendent, wanted this school. The details were in each organization's mind's eye. DCPS envisioned, I believe, a relief school in their own image that was on our campus and would operate just as other schools in the district. Since at that time our image was far from concrete, we left this meeting having to do the work of creating that image.

When faced with a blank slate, I assume most of the imaging is at the microlevel. My notes reflect these microissues, such as computer linkages to other schools, technology needs, community and parent integration, business involvement, teacher renewal, professionalization issues, in-service opportunities, year-round school, individualized educational programs, preschool, and so forth. None of these is related to the establishment of a permanent, sustainable, innovative collaboration. They are egocentric, just as the presumption of DCPS was to create a school that met its structural needs. The real work lay before us since we were not prepared to ask the questions that would move beyond the cognitive understandings we already historically had of working with another organization.

Not long after this meeting our contact person in DCPS left the county. A dialogue was beginning in the COE about the school. I met with the dean and suggested that we immediately establish a relationship with the person who would take over the project so as not to lose momentum. Time again was critical, and a publicly agreeable guideline for involvement was necessary, along with the establishment of a formal team at FIU to lead in the formulation of goals, organizational structure, and mission of the school. This would allow us to bring to the table early the direction we would like to see for a research facility on campus.

In September the college convened a "Dream Team" committee and invited persons external to the college to participate. Anyone who wanted to participate was welcome, and this opportunity to be a part of the process also became part of the problem as ideas would later be introduced and often not be compatible with others. But, the initiator of the idea would persist in advancing his or her own agenda disregarding the effect it had on other developing issues. By October we knew who in DCPS would be the contact person, and a meeting at the school district narrowed down some of the essential details of the school. Elementary school SSD-1 would be a prototype elementary facility, have a capacity of 885 students (since the footprint of the site was only five acres), and occupancy, according to the Advance Planning Division, would be January, 1995, with construction commencing in the summer of 1993. Obviously, none of this came to pass. What was a crisis of space at the time was confounded by a hurricane, which took precedence. Three months allotted for planning turned into three years, but the result is far different, I believe, than that which would have been possible if we adhered to the original schedule. Some of the ideas talked about at that meeting revolved around the ethnic makeup of the school. It seemed important at the time to balance the population so that it reflected the ethnicity of the county, even though the area is largely Hispanic. Also, we envisioned a birth to university perspective by this time, whereby services would be provided to children, parents, and community so that they could avail themselves of all the opportunities and services of a university environment.

We have here the beginning of the dialogue that pitted tradition, or rather each organization's conception of tradition, against innovation. The first conflict originated from the university, which issued an ultimatum of points that were negotiable and those that were non-negotiable. Control issues surfaced immediately as to selection of a principal and other personnel for the school, even before the ideology and mission of the school were determined. Assurance that the university would not be locked out of the decision making was deemed operational if the principal was a member of the faculty or jointly assigned to FIU and DCPS and that the lines of accountability for the operation of the school would circumvent the area superintendents and go directly to the superintendent and the president. This was not a realistic expectation.

A memo to the faculty invited anyone with an interest to join the Steering Committee and contribute ideas to the project. The language of the memo was to "allow yourself the greatest freedom and broadest latitude" in ideas. The memo also announced that in addition to the Steering Committee, three other groups were forming, that of building facilities and site committee, governance committee, and school theme, mission, and goals committee. This opened another area of contention because there was no macrolevel attempt until much later to assess whether ideas were compatible, consistent, legal, or politically viable. Instead, representatives from the university took non-negotiable points to DCPS who, appropriately from their perspective, took affront to most of them. By the time we left the meeting, we were talking about a multistory building with over 1,000 students with 80 percent of the population coming from local overcrowded schools, largely Hispanic, and 20 percent other. The principal, we were told, could not be affiliated with FIU because of union and contractual issues, and we were left with two issues that were resolved. The facility would have unlimited opportunity for experimentation, research, and teacher training, and the DCPS administration would allow this to occur.

At this time the participants began to talk about using this opportunity of joint planning to submit a proposal to the New American School Development Corporation to request funding related to then-president George Bush's America 2000 plan. This transference of point of view provided an opportunity to do some real macroplanning beyond the restrictions placed upon the project by the political agenda. The purpose of these proposals was to create a truly innovative school, and the funding possibility would alleviate all the microlevel detractors to innovation. Constant waiting and indecision can revert the process back to traditional action, which fills the void left by constant planning. Success requires transcendence of organizational and institutional concerns and personal agenda toward a common goal. This grant-writing project provided just the vehicle to aid the transformation.

I went ahead on my own and put together a proposal for a community-based program with the focus on family, which would remove the isolation of programs between health and social services, education, community school, and counseling through integration of services. The facility I envisioned was based on the school family as center of advocacy and integration of services. The full-time, year-round facility would meet the community needs and require a structure different from facilities that are top-down permission givers. This model would be a jointly held trust between the facilitating areas that impact on the education, health, and welfare of families, communities, and the children who live in them. I passed the plan on to the leaders of the grant committee and then presented it to a collective meeting to begin the formal process of working on the proposal for funding. My ideas were well received and created good dialogue between the university people and the large number of DCPS personnel at the meeting. Personally, this presentation provided entree to the people in DCPS that I would later be working with. Coming from a neighboring school system and being new to the university, I had no history with them and they did not know me. This turned out to be a positive, since in both organizations there were people who did not want to work with each other.

There followed, during the rest of 1991, the scramble of meetings to accommodate the January, 1992 deadline for the proposal. As the structure was elaborated, clarity of dimensions of micro/macro planning began to unfold. Ideas had to be realistically implementable, and the connectivity of one dream had to be fully thought out in relationship to the others. Some of the ideas generated became a firm part of the newly created collective vision and made their way from the grant proposal to be part of the understood areas of agreement concerning the school on campus. The meetings also provided opportunity for new players from FIU to interact with DCPS, myself included.

The title of the proposal that was submitted to the New American Schools for funding was "Interdependence Through Shared Empowerment." Because it set the stage for the school proposal that was finally agreed upon, looking back at the importance of this as setting the tone for the future is clearly warranted. By interdependence and shared empowerment, DCPS, FIU, the union, the community college, and the Chamber of Commerce symbolically made a pact that what was being designed was different from what existed before. The presumption was that the stakeholders, the parents, students, teachers, school administrators, and the community at large, could be empowered from the framework of a comprehensive, innovative delivery system. This empowerment would take the form of full participation in a process of reform. There were five elements of this proposal. The first was to support education by the development of a school community that would provide linkages and support for education. This component was essentially that of the presentation I had made to the group when we began the process of working on the proposal. Second was the preschool and community programs that involve parents, community, businesses, and social agencies. Third was a redesigned curriculum, thematic, interdisciplinary, with multi-age flexible grouping, and activity-based geared toward academic success. Fourth was a teacher-training component, which is substantial and continuing with support from the larger community. Fifth was a new governance pattern for decision making.

We made the final list of thirty, but the funding source for the New American Schools did not raise enough money to fully implement what they had projected, and our project was cut. But, there was mostly positive dialogue among the participants, especially between those on the team for the new school on campus. While efforts were directed toward the proposal, little was done formally to work on the campus school. We, instead, were hoping for external funding, so we fell back into the microdecisions that were peripheral to the conceptions of mission for the school. Without external funding, we could not hope to implement the school envisioned by the proposal as it was written. The reality was that, without the extra funds, we had to redesign the school within the confines of what was feasible, practical, and possible for each of the primary organizations.

The Transition Period: To Build or Not to Build

The book of state restrictions and specifications on building schools is a complex of materials that are deciphered best by architects and engineers, not by university personnel or curriculum specialists. We spent the good part of the beginning of 1992 discussing site plans while the planners from each organization did their own communicating. All these preliminary discussions concerned feasibility of site selection, terms of the lease, and the unusual footprint of the site on a five-acre pie-shaped lot. We endlessly discussed parking, access, and buses. We also visited a number of schools in Dade and Broward counties hoping that attention to the details of construction would complement the vision we had of what this school would need to operate. Form follows function, Frank Lloyd Wright notwithstanding, and must proceed from an idea of what it is that drives choices so that the facility serves the goals of the school. Of course at this time we envisioned the New America School version of this vision—that of a community-based, family-centered facility. But, we had not narrowed down any of the details of how that family-based school would operate. We also thought, at least the university did, that there would be more flexibility in the design than was ultimately possible. The final lease agreement, as approved by each organization and their lawyers, did not reach its final version until 1995, after the architect was chosen! The final result of these discussions was that with minor adaptations, the prototype DCPS school was more economical and could be built faster, especially since speed of construction was important. It also was a state-of-the-art facility, more than adequate for the needs and vision of this school as finally adopted. The architect was selected through standard Dade County procedures, without input from us. Although symbolically this was a loss to our participation, the reality was that we had agreed to the prototype, and they were procedurally following their time agenda as defined and operationalized by them. Our holistic vision of the elements coming together at once with full participation by our team at each step along the way was just not the reality of the way their organization managed such procedures. They were bound by legal restrictions and affirmative action policies, and some players on our team needed to come to understand that those things would not and could not change.

This aspect of lease agreement would later prove to be an important external influence on the school development process. This site was only one of a larger land agreement going on between the university, the school system, and metro Dade County; the delays

were less about the school site than about the agreements and process of the larger land exchange. Therefore, before we could go ahead
and finish the proposal to go to the School Board, we had to have
the agreed upon lease signed. That was delayed by external nonpar-
ticipants in the school project because of other agendas, which were
largely political. Knowledge of this came much later when we discovered that the delay was repeatedly from our end, not, as we had
supposed, from the school system. Also, when the lawyers started to
participate in the lease agreement details, the process bogged down
and became the back-and-forth delivering of minor changes in wording of the agreement of which we had no knowledge. Through March,
1995—three years into the process described in this narrative—the
lawyers were still sending the document, slowly, back and forth.

In March of 1992, the university team was charged by the dean
to proceed with the project suggesting that it be open to everyone at
the college who had an interest in participating and that we fully
organize, create a time line, and establish a continuing relationship
with DCPS and the union. Over the next two years, repeatedly,
team members would meet at the dean's initiation and discuss whether
we should continue the project, usually when the negotiations seemed
stalled. There comes a time in all negotiations when there is no turn-
ing back, even if the microaspects are not going the way you planned.
This doesn't mean that the project has failed. What is gained should
not be measured by a linear yardstick, because what we were after
ultimately was a new way of working with each other, and this went
beyond the creation of the school. On a personal level, this threat of
stopping the project, which I had worked on for so long, was extremely frustrating and stressful. It appeared that when things got
too difficult, like children playing a game, our administration's response was to back off and take our toys home rather than trying to
work things out. Building an atmosphere of trust to support collaboration is difficult when in the back of your mind is the idea that
if the other side does not do what we want, we will withdraw and
forget the whole thing. The consequences of playing this kind of
game are devastating. The other side learns that what we say has
nothing to do with the way we act.

In response, an April meeting was set up and, to provide structure for the discussion, I prepared a listing of areas for decision mak-

ing and negotiation, which was to be handed out. Meetings typically from this point on included DCPS people, COE team members, and union and parent representation. Sites were alternated between DCPS administrative office and the college campus. Formality and informality, even whether participants took off their jackets and rolled up their sleeves, were gauges to detect whether decisions would be made or whether the meeting was for posturing. By setting the agenda in advance, the list I created formed the focus of this meeting and the branching out of discussion on how to proceed. We talked about the makeup of the advisory for the school and the importance of including business and community participants. The structure and organization of the administration concerned issues of selection, staffing, liaison to the university, and the form of shared decision making that would continue the relationship to the College of Education. Curriculum and evaluation issues and formative and summative design and implementation with an eye on accountability and achievement were discussed. University access for research, experimentation, teacher training, and dissemination was another major theme. Policy issues of year-round school and extended day would be brought up, accepted, rejected, and brought up again repeatedly. Student demographics and grant writing to obtain funding for our wish list were also considered.

Our committee met to discuss once again the architectural considerations for the school. Before we had a conception of the school on paper, we kept coming back to the microneeds of the facility, especially those participants who had elementary experience. Space was a big concern—planning areas, removable walls, two-way mirrors, office space for faculty from the university (which was not positively embraced by DCPS), and a large indoor area for developmental physical education. In total we made a list of seventeen architectural elements deemed essential. This focus was brought to the next meeting of the larger group, and we spent the entire time talking about decision making in an area we really had very little to say about. Parking, footprints, leases, classroom restrictions, cafeteria space, architectural details, and construction specifications didn't make this process seem so innovative or empowering.

I found in my notes from this time a reference to Guba and Lincoln (1989, 149–150), who described evaluative processes as being hermeneutic and dialectic and needing to have minimum requirements. Each side must work from a position of integrity. The participants must have the competence to communicate and a willingness to share power and change beliefs. They must also reconsider value positions and make commitments of time and energy to the process. None of this was going on as we endlessly talked about the site itself. This was a nine million dollar construction project, and little attention was being paid to what would go on inside the building once it was finished. Isn't this why we got involved in the first place? The opportunity to create a school responsive to student populations, innovative and experimental in curriculum and delivery, was becoming secondary to the negotiation process and the endless details of what could and could not happen. It was almost as if there was a planned subversion of the goals that had brought us together in the first place—a subversion at the expense of the work we were trying to create and the collective culture that was fighting to emerge. We were still talking about staffing, decision-making structures, dividing the student body into three communities, and staffing concerns when the superintendent assigned one of their team members to be the official contact person for DCPS.

Several concerns about the process were surfacing. From our perspective, since we still were operating from an isomorphic perspective, questions were not being addressed that would meet our perceived needs. I wrote a memo to the associate dean who was also a member of the committee. Basically, the questions posed in the memo were about protecting us and our organization: What kinds of administrative structure would meet our needs? What are our needs? Are they to maintain control and decision making of the project? To redefine the COE? To create a research facility at the school? To support innovation? Can the goals of the program be congruent with the goals of the COE? Another set of questions was about the collaboration itself: How can we mediate and protect ourselves from the DCPS hierarchy of permission givers and the top-down decision-making structure? Who do we want to answer to? What waivers can we anticipate needing so that we have access to the school? Do we need to anticipate all our needs or can we create a flexible structure? A third set of questions was more general concerns that needed answers internally: Who needs to buy-in to the project? How? What support do we have internally and externally, and what support can we expect?

In order to move away from the endless discussions of site concerns and on to more workable areas, I gave the dean a list of issues concerning the school that could not be addressed by the committee. These issues had to be addressed by the lawyers and administration of the university since they included site size, which was beginning to look like an unsurmountable problem. DCPS had asked that the agreed upon 885 student population of the school be expanded to 1,000 housed in a multistory facility that would require more land than the proposed five acres. We had repeatedly discussed the research that supports student achievement and success related to school size. Everyone agreed that a smaller school was not only desirable, but also in the best interests of the students and their families, which probably would largely be immigrant. DCPS, on the other hand, had a real concern with and a growing problem of overcrowded schools in the area that clearly needed relief. Our noneducative concern was the large number of elementary students who would be utilizing some of the campus facilities and our own problems with overcrowding and space. Since this school population would be fully transported by bus, access needed to be addressed as did parking for staff. Lastly, could the physical education facilities of FIU be used by the school since there was no room to build on the site? We took my list to the provost, who agreed to find out the answers to these questions and communicate them to DCPS. So, our site-planning committee started to communicate with theirs, our administration with theirs, and we hoped that the committee work would move forward to the issues of policy and practice that would define the school itself.

The policy issues concerned administration and governance, site specifications that would support the design conception, and student demographics and balance. The maintenance of cultural integrity of the two organizations was starting to emerge, and while speaking to the dean I began to look at the project as two triangles that overlap. A separate triangle represented the structure of each organization, but the bottom angles of these two triangles were starting to overlap in the personal exchanges people were having with each other. This new sphere of operation would later expand, and, when possible, separate entirely from the formal structure of each parent organization. This idea was the precursor to the transorganizational alliance discussed in Chapter 2.

Then came Hurricane Andrew, which not only brought the community together, but also personalized the process for many of the players. Out of chaos came the need to plan, but also out of chaos came other priorities for DCPS and for the participants who had lost their homes or faced months of displacement and reconstruction. The school became less urgent, but this gave us the time needed to create something more substantial in the end.

Chapter Five
Negotiations:
Power, Authority, and Truth

The development of a community can result from an intervention that goes against the norms of convention. The normal operations are transformed through abnormal interactions that emanate from positions of authority, power, and conceptions of truth. The emergence of new forms follows from discourse, the playing out of strategies, the overcoming of resistance, and the planned efforts of those with knowledge and ability to create an overall effort of change. Discussions about the dialogues and the agenda of each organization can create opportunities that may lead to the alteration of how the institution sees itself (Martusewica, 1992, 147).

Change is a struggle between the reinforcing of existing processes that balance and stabilize and the new through the use of feedback and analysis (Senge, 1990, 79). Complications can be meliorated by understanding the multiplicity of advocacy, creation of new dependencies of team members in each organization, development of new regulatory controls, and creation of values that break from tradition and are situationally driven.

The impetus for change can be both internal and external. Often the external influences are based on rumors and half-truths that create perceptions that impede progress through pressure or influence impacting on intergroup dynamics. Knowledge—and the withholding of knowledge—also is an element of power wielding. The giving and taking of information and the awareness of the source of positioning of members of each group are critical components in implementing a change effort. Players cannot act in isolation. This serves only to reinforce and perpetuate traditional beliefs and behavior. Information must be made public, at least to the agent directing the process. Disclosure and discourse are not enough either. Analysis for meaning and interpretation of resulting behavior are constantly forming and reforming perspective and provide the methodology for future resolution of conflict and an action orientation. Knowledge of what came before gives insight into the present. Without this constant sifting of knowledge, interpretation is not valid.

Exchange of knowledge exists in two forms. First is what is said openly and shared, which Argyris and Schon (1974) called espoused theories. Public declaration of position is common, and people interact with each other mostly based on the openly declared statements of each. The theories in use, however, are those behaviors that are consistent or at odds with the declared theories of practice. Over time, if the theories in use are different from the espoused theories, distrust and uncertainty cloud the interactions between players. Taken to the level of the organization, when organizations espouse collegiality and collaboration but behave in ways to thwart the actualization, a sound basis of future interactions is just not a realistic expectation. Behaviors that match espoused theories pave the way for a playing field that is open to new ideas and means of operation. It also is open to enabling linkages outside the organization.

In June of 1992, the espoused positions representing policy issues of concern to the two organizations in this study were not congruent in three major areas: administration and governance, site configuration, and demographics. Significant is the relative distance between the two positions represented in the chart that follows. Although both sides were talking about (espousing) negotiations and compromise, the behaviors were not consistent (theories in use). In particular, administration and governance reflect the COE position that we be included and participatory. The DCPS position was that this be a DCPS run and operated school, by the book. Site configuration, on which we would spend a large portion of our time, was a tug-of-war over what each side wanted and who would pay for it if it went beyond that which normally was provided by a prototype school. Demographic positioning was clear. DCPS espoused a non-negotiable position that the school be a relief school. At no time did their theories in use conflict with their espoused position. FIU, on the other hand, dreamed that this school would be demographically reflective of the larger Dade County makeup when to do so really posed many more problems than were feasible and no one came up with viable ways to make this espoused idea a reality.

Administration and Governance:
How shall the school be governed?

FIU/COE Position	DCPS Position
• An advisory (led by FIU designees and DCPS designees) would report to the area superintendent and function as a governing body	Governance by area superintendent
• The advisory will select the principal who may be a member of the COE's faculty, a DCPS employee eligible for faculty appointment, but jointly selected	DCPS employee jointly selected
• The principal will be selected 12 months before the school opens	Selected 6 months before the school opens
• Staff will be selected by a joint committee of COE and DCPS	
• The elementary school may, in conjunction with the advisory, make final decisions on such factors as extended day, year-round school, new evaluation criteria, and make curricular decisions, such as non-tracked, thematic integration, etc.	DCPS administrative sequence of approval
• The COE will have access to the school for research, urban teacher training	DCPS research approval process
• The COE will maintain technology linkages connecting the school with offices and laboratories in the college	
• Action research not limited to but including methodologies and materials as a matter of course	

Site: How shall the site be configured?

FIU/COE Position	DCPS Position
Site size of 5 acres cannot support a DCPS committed to a 885 student population school with projections of opening with over 1,000 students. *A smaller school would comfortably be housed on 5 acres (500 or less).*	885 student population school, over 1,000 when it opens Who has the responsibility for site preparation?

This influences the following:

• Site design must be at least two stories to accommodate student body	Site of 5 acres is not sufficient
• Can FIU provide parking for school staff?	Must come from FIU
• Access for cars and buses must be provided for a 100% transported school population	Access on FIU property in addition to 5 acres
• Can there be joint use of FIU facilities (i.e., for physical education, music, art, classroom space) to expand space restrictions in the elementary school?	Joint use needed due to space restrictions

Site specifications include:

• Space to house faculty (offices)	Prototype school
• Three distinct community spaces	
• Community school organization and space	
• Technology linkup for networking to College of Education, etc.	
• Preschool	
• Observation areas for research	

Demographics: **What shall be the student population of the school?**

FIU/COE Position	*DCPS Position*
If the school is primarily a relief school, its racial and ethnic makeup will not mirror the broader community.	Relief school largely Hispanic
Can we reexplore the possibility of including the children of FIU employees to bring the balance back to a reflection of the county demographics?	

By September of 1992, clarification of these three areas of concern came from a meeting between the president of the university, the superintendent, and the provost. The resolution included the following working principles, which would guide the process. The principal of the school would be brought in early to assist in planning, and FIU would be involved in the selection. FIU agreed to provide the five acres of land for the school and joint use could be made of the surrounding fields for playground space. The size of the school would be capped at 885. The architect, commissioned by DCPS, would work with FIU who would have final sign-off on the structure of the building (we were in a phase of other building construction and I suspect that the cohesiveness of the vision of the campus was what prompted this item). The superintendent agreed that the principal would report to the head of the Office of Instructional Leadership. The budget for building the school was determined to be approximately $9 million. The plant itself could possibly have three floors, and underground parking would be investigated.

More importantly for the committee participants, it was agreed that the philosophy of the school would jointly be developed by FIU and DCPS and that the supporting committees would include appointed individuals from business, PTA, union, DCPS, and FIU. A smaller design team, the Steering Committee, would do the majority of the groundwork with representatives from Dade County and FIU. I was designated as the chair of the team. As it turned out, I became cochair with an associate dean from the College of Education. I understood that this was an attempt to protect my untenured status from those who perceived that they should have the title. The other members of this committee representing FIU were from elementary education and physical education. Full participation from all departments in the College of Education would come through subcommittee membership. Two members of this committee, myself included, were nontenured assistant professors who, in some respects, were taking a risk participating in a project that may not be valuable toward tenure earning. (Time-intensive projects detract from time used for presentations and publications, and the tenure system is traditionally geared to measure success by orthodoxy.)

The official minutes from the first Steering Committee meeting with the appointed members listed an agenda item for the creation of a time line for completion of the proposal. The format was to follow that of a Saturn Proposal, a DCPS format used to apply for innovative new schools. The second item on the agenda was division into subcommittees to work on the formal part of writing a proposal. After once again discussing the site plan, this area was removed from group responsibility as the lease agreement now was in the hands of the attorneys, or so we thought. We reviewed the principles the memorandum described and then a representative from

DCPS Labor Relations talked to us about waivers that might be needed or interagency agreements and approvals from varied interest groups. The last item of the day was a schedule for subsequent task force meetings and the subcommittees, which needed to be established to prepare the written proposal. These included the areas of curriculum and instruction, physical plant, school organization, community linkages, and research.

There appeared to be a real difference in the atmosphere of this meeting. DCPS personnel were less cautious, more open in their recommendations; there was an atmosphere of "we can work it out" and a feeling that compromises were within reach. They seemed excited about the prospect of working on a joint collaboration for the first time since this process began, and the idea of documenting the negotiation process as research was agreeable. They did not want, however, the meetings to be tape-recorded. FIU people were also more generous in their approach, and there was a give and take on both sides.

As we would do repeatedly, our members and anyone interested in participating attended a pre-Steering Committee meeting. It was important to our cochairs to work out our position prior to airing what would possibly be taken as internal conflicts at the larger committee meeting. Perceptions are everything. The nature of our professorial work is that differing points of view are the stuff on which we thrive. What appears to be lack of unity or conformity to others is the nature of our individual fields of expertise. The result of this meeting was a clear analysis of each of the five areas of the written proposal. We included as many elements of further discussion, description, and decision making as we could think of and I put them into chart format. This form was passed out at the next Steering Committee meeting, and it formed the basis of the discussion. I told the committee that physical plant and teacher training areas seemed to permeate all other areas. It was evident there were areas of difference of perspective in some of the categories. We discussed thematic integration, birth to prekindergarten focus, technology, year-round education, shared decision making, class size, school structure and staff selection, physical plant lending itself to three communities, community linkages, research procedures, and inclusion of university faculty or students' children attending the school. It was a very productive dialogue. The research area was the most positively received. It really is the area that delineates the uniqueness and commitment of the university to the project. Discussion centered around teacher training, advanced degree courses offered on site, research and dissemination, and involvement of preservice teachers at the school.

The Steering Committee decided to create an expanded committee at this time, with subcommittees and their own chairs to work out the details of each of the five areas on the worksheet. Each area would have two Steering Committee members as cochairs, one from DCPS and one from FIU. DCPS would advise those selected from the community (parents, the union, etc.) and school system as to their membership on the committees, and FIU would request participation from all those who were interested, encouraging those identified as having critical expertise in an area. A full meeting of all of the participants was scheduled for November, 1992 at the university for a kick-off rally. We could now even give the project a name, which we did at the kick-off.

This decision-making meeting was openly cooperative. The men took off their jackets and rolled up their sleeves. We talked about who and what was possible and why! The chairs from each side started to form a new connection. The restrictions and barriers to collaborating began to have less rigid walls.

To ensure full access to participation and to inform the faculty in the COE of the process as it unfolded, I presented a project update to the October Faculty Assembly meeting, gave out the Steering Committee minutes, and distributed the worksheet for input. This was also distributed to faculty not in attendance. I specifically asked the faculty at this meeting to think about how teacher training and faculty involvement could permeate throughout the proposal and the extent of their willingness to contribute, and in what form, as university, college, and individual faculty.

The organizational structure of the school system determined the decision-making process, which is hierarchical and top-down. For the university, even though it appears to be hierarchical, there is equal legitimacy to influence from the bottom-up (as described in

Chapter 2). Therefore, it was important that everyone have knowledge of and an opportunity to participate in the design of and future access to the school.

The direction and tone of interaction in the COE is set by the dean. His method of operation is through consensus building whereby all participants have an opportunity to be equal partners. This process is often unwieldy since participants come in and out of a process almost at will and must catch up to others or cause issues previously put to rest to be brought up again and again with new proposals for resolution. The COE has often been publicly opposed to the school system solutions with the public school thinking COE is in an ivory tower with little real contact with the problems faced by public education. Faculty views, although sound and based on research, either personal or adopted, do not take into account the ramifications of the day-to-day operation of a school. They don't see the domino effect of their recommendations, and often an idea is generated in isolation of other equally valid perspectives. Therefore, DCPS seems to put the university through a trial-by-fire of participation based on our performance in formal and informal contacts.

I am sensitive to this because my experience prior to being a faculty member was with a neighboring school system. Some faculty do not have a lot of empathy for the reality of school life. They don't fully appreciate the complexity of an ever-changing environment, so that, when they make suggestions for inclusion in the proposal, they do not see all that must occur to implement or question whether a public school system is equipped to make the changes proposed. There is a cost involved in faculty involvement and volunteerism. COE faculty bring expertise, which may or may not be legitimate, but they also bring criticism. When made vocal, perceptions become ingrained, and individuals in the school system learn whom they want to deal with and whom they don't. Their selection of whom to interact with is not made based on agreement per se, I believe, but on legitimate and respectful interchanges of opinion. They rightly object to being preached at since they view themselves as having as much expertise as the university faculty.

On November 13, 1992, the kick-off meeting was held at FIU. I prepared an updated version of the five categories (Worksheet #1), and DCPS prepared a contact list of participants and chairs of the

WORKSHEET #1
FIU College of Education/Dade County
Public Schools

Curriculum and Instruction
Thematic Integration
Evaluation: portfolio,
   continuous progress, testing
Non-tracked
Learning Styles
Multicultural
Family-Centered Education
Activity-Based Education
Birth to Prekindergarten Focus
Technology in the Curriculum
	Physical Plant
	Three Communities (K–1, 1–3, 3–5)
	Community Access
	Technology/Media
	Faculty Space (offices)
	Observation Areas
	Flexible Use of Facilities: large,
	   open, air-conditioned, multiple
	   use spaces

School Organization/Policy
Yearly, Daily Schedule
School Structure and Selection:
   Principal, Assistant Principal,
   Lead Teacher; Community;
   Teaching Staff, Support Staff;
   Preschool Staff; Liaison to
   Community School
Site-Based Planning
Shared Decision-Making Model
Relationship with COE
Class Size (student/adult ratio)
	Community Linkages
	Family/Community School
	Counseling
	Services
	Linkages, Integration of Services
	Preschool

University Research Component
Teacher Preparation: urban teacher training, activity-based,
   technology, parent/community
   involvement, preservice teachers in school
Research/Experimentation: culture of research
Access by COE Professors: faculty involvement in the school
Technology Linkages
Resource Sharing: access to FIU facilities
Dissemination
Grant Writing
In-service
Teachers in the School: working on advanced degrees, working as
   adjuncts
Principal Having a Role in Our Institution
Laboratory Setting

subcommittees. They also gave the project a working title and brought it to the meeting: "Co-STAAR, Collaborative School to Achieve Academic Restructuring." It is interesting that the term *collaboration* became part of the title of the project. I wondered what that meant to them and what it meant to us. How would it be operationalized so it would not fall into the patterns of the past in which collaboration was a fleeting, momentary project that participants joined together for, but when the project was over, they moved on? These projects do not have any lasting impact on either organization and produce no systemic changes in the way each operates or views its roles and responsibilities. At this meeting, DCPS provided the opening remarks; I gave a summary of how the Steering Committee derived the five categories and why the participants were asked to attend and what their mission was. The group divided into the five workgroups and we circulated around the room clarifying points under each category. We gave the groups a time line for completion of their work by March 1, 1993, and asked them to meet before winter break and provide us with a schedule so that a member of the Steering Committee could attend all meetings.

This was an exciting meeting. Representatives from both organizations, the union, parents and other branches of the university were working together to create something new. We asked that each group keep minutes and that they be passed on to the Steering Committee through the chairs of the subcommittees. Privately, the DCPS Steering Committee leader and I talked about how the proposal could have been written solely by the design team, but the diversity of the constituency of the subcommittees was so important to future acceptance by the school board that this became a valuable experience. We also spoke about the special interests that each board member represented (multicultural, the arts, exceptional education, health services, academics) and how they voted from their own perspectives.

My notes about this meeting caution that our participants be careful that school personnel not dominate the process by sheer numbers. Each of our subcommittee cochairs was asked to participate fully in the design and details of each group. It was also obvious that each team's work would produce much more than was needed for a final proposal. The essence of each of their written parts would have to be edited into a comprehensive whole by the Steering Committee. That process would be a collaborative effort if the interventions created by this project changed the way each organization viewed the other. I understood that this effort was the experiment and that success was the continuance of participation and influence. The school system still viewed this school as representing a continuance of structural integrity and maintenance of accountability, which were to be perpetuated no matter what the details of the final proposal. Given this perspective, when one side made waves over details that were as yet even to be fully described by subcommittee or Steering Committee, the other tended to pull back and question whether the project should continue. This came from the university and college administration. Consensus, as seen by the detractors, was agreement. For me, the dialogue always kept open possibilities and as long as the major players understood each other and the position and influences upon them, then the dialogue was open. If this transformed into the wielding of power and influence, or the holding and withholding of authority and rewards, the process would break down. So, the Steering Committee members had to guard against this and start building bridges between members that would persist and rise above the naysayers. Meanwhile, the subcommittee work proceeded, minutes were taken, and exciting linkages continued to form between members of varied groups.

We moved into the year 1993 foreseeing that we were proceeding on schedule and that it would not be long before the subcommittee work would finish and the Steering Committee could put the final proposal together for the various approvals necessary. This was more than optimistic as outside influences continued to impact on the process and delays continuously plagued the work.

The Steering Committee, including the union representative, met in January to review the progress of each of the subcommittees. Naturally the meeting began with a report of where we were regarding the lease. The superintendent and the president of the university were corresponding and responding, and the letters would be made available to us soon. The nature of the discussion now was on access to surrounding areas beyond the five-acre, two-story school. The letter from the superintendent talked of an "encouraging sign that we are well on the road to fruition in this cooperative venture" and listed the following criteria for continuance, although the language tried to put to rest DCPS concerns. The letter listed, in essence, those areas that were not negotiable if we wanted to continue:

1. The size of the plot to be leased . . . will be five acres.

2. The maximum number of students to be assigned to the school will be 885, with the understanding that the school is being established as a relief school for students in overcrowded schools in the area.

3. The budget for constructing the school will be capped at $9 million, with no provision for overruns.

4. The architect commissioned by DCPS to work with FIU will follow all procedural and other requirements of the DCPS.

5. In the event that the school to be constructed will need to include a third floor, it will have to be designed and intended for instructional purposes only.

6. The DCPS, in consultation with FIU, will have the final sign-off on the structure of the building.

7. DCPS and FIU will develop a joint agreement on the philosophy of the school, such philosophy being consistent with and supportive of the goals of the DCPS.

8. The principal of the school will be selected following procedures established by the School Board rule, however, a request will be made of the School Board which would allow one (1) person from FIU to participate in the interviews and selection process. Principals will be allowed to apply for a lateral transfer to the school. If a lateral transfer is not accepted, the interview and selection process, from the qualified candidate roster, will be followed.

9. The principal selected will be assigned to the school six months prior to the anticipated opening of the school, following established DCPS procedures for the staffing of a Saturn-type school.

10. The principal assigned to the school will be administratively responsible to the region superintendent, following established DCPS procedures.

Each subcommittee chair gave a report on the progress of each of the committees at the Steering Committee session. Summaries of their work to date follow:

The Curriculum and Instruction committee reported that the group had reviewed the competencies for elementary grades. Each member was charged to present an overview of what is current in their area of expertise. Some commonalities emerged from the individual presentations. These were critical-thinking and higher-order skills, alternative assessment, higher standards, and accelerated schools. The end product is expected to be a set of general standards for curriculum. Each individual was paired with an individual from the other organization by subject area expertise to write their section of the proposal.

Physical Plant committee members visited two schools and felt that they must wait to see the other committees' written work before finishing their task since many physical plant decisions depend on elements from the other areas.

The School Organization committee reported that this group met once and wants to meet with the curriculum committee. They will address the community aspect within the school and nongraded progress. It is a given that shared decision making and principal accountability would be elements in the final proposal, but the choices include members of the decision-making group being built into the proposal, cadre or advisory, organization, staffing, replacement of teachers after initial staffing, transfers, interviewing, and surplus teachers. After three subsequent meetings, this group produced a noncomprehensive product. They viewed this area as predetermined in that the selected principal and staff would traditionally be charged with the choices after they were selected. As it turned out, this provided the opportunity later for the most innovative aspect of this project to occur. Not creating the focus for shared decision making left it up to those of us on the Steering Committee to look at what was innovative and take the steps necessary to try something new here. But, this turn of events came later.

The Community Linkages committee reported that this group focused on the America 2000 community component, and participants were given areas to research. Among the areas they were evaluating were library access, adult education, GED, new immigrant educational services, an agency liaison position, women and infant education, job training, transportation services, a multicultural center, business and corporate support and training workshops, community school, and adult education outreach satellite center for ESOL (English for Speakers of Other Languages) and parent education.

The University Research group reported that they were exploring cooperative action research and involvement of faculty. The larger group discussed involvement of preservice students to reduce the student–teacher ratio.

The Steering Committee then discussed the possibility of a longer school day for students, a staggered day for teachers, and the opportunity to provide for-credit classes at the site for post–service recertification and for retraining, as well as for degree-seeking students. The complexity of the process led the Steering Committee to postpone the completion date of all subcommittee work for one month. The plan then was to have all work reviewed by the Steering Committee with the final draft distributed to the COE faculty, DCPS, and union people prior to final copy and presentation to the School Board.

Issues of power, authority, and control kept resurfacing even at the most cooperative stages of this project. DCPS people were more privy to the exchanges of the superintendent and university president than COE people were. So, in a formal meeting they would tell us about us. Also, they attempted to include every innovation in one site and talked about every innovation as equally possible, which is inappropriate. I brought this up during the meeting and questioned whether conceptually and programmatically all the cliches of authentic assessment, portfolios, accountability, critical thinking, and so forth really do go together and can be, or should be, implemented at one site. This was a difficult discussion to have with them. The 1990s are both a good and a bad time to be in public education. On the one hand, every innovation has a legitimacy and is able to be implemented. On the other hand, the measure of success of each innovation is still achievement and standardized test scores, comparative in nature. Innovations that may negate results of each due to incompatibility are implemented, often at one site; or, innovations that have successes not measured by standardized scores are continued or terminated on the basis of inappropriate measures. Sometimes we just don't wait long enough for the innovation to make a difference in the tested measures. Internal problems were also apparent. The elements of the proposal were starting to look as if they would require a large commitment on the part of the university staff for effective implementation. Questions about faculty involvement and credit toward tenure or promotion for involvement would have to be discussed early in the process to keep the momentum and interest in participation. If the answers were not formalized, the impetus for involvement might not continue.

In January of 1993 each of the groups met and started to work out the details of what would eventually be in their section of the proposal. The community linkage group explored the full-service school concept. They were interested in integrating education, medical, and/or social and human services that are beneficial to meeting the needs of children, youth, and their families on the school grounds or in other easily accessible locations. Another aspect under consideration was the integration of school programs with the ongoing student programs at the university. These included after school programs to be provided and administered through the Department of Health, Physical Education, and Recreation with graduate and undergraduate students implementing the programs while earning credits.

In February I went to Taiwan to teach. While I was away DCPS responded to the ten-point letter from our president, and they took exception to some of the points. Specifically they could not fund a principal for more than six months prior to the opening of the school. The other point was that overruns in construction would be capped. This seemed a reasonable budgetary concern and a planning problem that could be worked out with support from the university personnel who could continue the preopening process until the principal could come on board. Our side, as it would do repeatedly, saw this as an obstacle and another moment when we would have to choose whether we wanted to continue. My response was that it depended not on DCPS, but on FIU/COE staff and what we were willing to offer. Details such as this are not that critical when taken in context of the entire project. The opportunity to make a difference and share a commitment to change—the macroelements of the effort—were far more important than the microdetails that are really not that significant until a later time. The process is the reality, and making a difference on an interpersonal level between the constituencies of each is the value of this project. It is not control. It is the creation of a process that is win-win for both organizations. Investment and respect are by-products at this time, and if they repeatedly over time interact positively with us, the resultant trust will be people to people, not the system and its limitations.

Involvement is an interesting phenomenon. The beginning of a project such as this engenders a lot of interest and involvement. The middle period of work requires sustained commitment, especially in a project with an ever-changing completion date. There are also people who want to be included and feel that they rightly have a say and stake in the project after it is ongoing for a period of time. These players seem to come out of the woodwork and offer different perspectives from those conceptually agreed upon by the larger group. The reverse also happens when certain players are needed to engender full participation, and then are too busy with other work to participate. Manifested also are those who observe without participating and then criticize from an external vantage point. There is a delicate balance between the wants and needs of each of the two organizations in this study, but there are also varying wants and needs within and between the departments and persons in the COE. DCPS is a less fluid environment. The individuals from DCPS know what they want and how to achieve the goal. Selection for participation is not voluntary but by assignment. The community and union players also are representative participants. Only the COE people are voluntary and less governed by rules and roles of responsibility. This is tied into the concept of service and the tenure and promotion process I talked about earlier. Commitment and support for staff involvement of a project such as this still had not been defined.

The COE sent me to attend a meeting in Tallahassee concerning developmental research schools. The laboratory schools in the state had been designated quasi school districts through legislation and were forming a network to share resources and disseminate research. The administration of the COE felt that this somehow would be leverage on our part if we had a fallback position if DCPS insisted on items that we could not agree to. Our administration thought that they were wielding power. I did not think so since the items changed in the ten-point memorandum were very reasonable and not conceptually influencing the project. They basically had to do with availability of money, and that was not inappropriate. My perspective was that we needed certain things from the development of this school, including the ability to go in and do research, have an open door, participate in the conception and possibly governance structure of the school, have student practicums there, and have faculty involved—wasn't that enough? But, our plans had to fit in and be cognizant of the way the public school system operated and did its work. If not, we would continue to be at odds with them over details, which were reflections merely of the way that they operate. When the school is built, we will have not only accomplished something significant, but also we will be survivors—survivors of the negotiations, as people who are welcome to come in and participate in the day-to-day goings-on of the school and be respected for our opinion and advice. If we don't want to be involved in the day-to-day operation of the school, then let us take on what we can handle and simply create a sphere of influence emanating from our expertise.

Much of my perspective comes from my field of curriculum. I believe that certain elements of curriculum and instructional planning must be considered and taken into account in the design in order to produce a holistic programmatically appropriate environment for teaching and learning. The elements are classical areas of sequence, balance, relevance, continuity, articulation, integration, and transferability. Therefore, when the particulars of the committee work started to come in for review, I felt that it was important to consider these elements so that the final proposal would be a cohesive whole, not merely a conglomeration of every new term and experiment in the field combined together at one site. The parts also had to fit realistically into how schools operate and how the proposed pieces fit together. The groups also tended to wander off into the areas being developed by other groups.

For example, the draft of the Curriculum Committee was compartmentalized into subject areas. Math, science, foreign language, ESOL, physical education, language arts, music, and a learning style section each presented their own philosophy for inclusion in the school. This would later have to be organized and edited so as to present a cohesive curriculum position. The Community Linkages group synthesized their work into a few pages describing services and activities for community support, parental awareness, educational involvement, and a structure of support services. From the perspective of the university, there was a great deal of cooperative planning in this area with offerings of university students and faculty support of programs. These included recreation, sports and movement activity programs, after school, evenings, and Saturday supervised by faculty and graduate and undergraduate students for course credit; adult and family programs and activities through the division of student affairs; career workshops for parents and families; orientation programs for family members returning to university; psycho educational workshops for parents and children, multicultural events and programs for parents and children; mentoring programs; free or low-cost admission to student affairs sponsored events; wellness programs; in school and after school activities and programs provided by faculty and graduate students from the College of Health; tutoring services for children, parents, and families by student clubs and organizations; and university library access for students and families.

In February of 1993, the Florida Commission on Education Reform and Accountability was charged with overseeing the creation of an outcome-based education system, which gives local schools and advisories the authority to determine how students meet performance standards. The local school districts were asked to look toward the collection of performance data for the seven goals that schools were expected to achieve, a time line for implementation of a school improvement process, and the utilization of a scheme for current assessment methods (Diegmueller, 1993). This initiative was to impact on the proposal for this school since DCPS had designed a competency-based curriculum that would meet the criteria of the reform movement and its emphasis on local control. The curriculum that they developed detailed the grade level subject area competencies that would drive successful student performance. It also would later impact on the curriculum section of the proposal.

By the deadline of April, 1993 for subcommittee work to be completed, only the physical plant group and research group had not distributed a draft. A meeting of the Steering Committee was set up for April, and the university participants decided to prepare a draft of the subcommittee work to bring to the table beforehand (again not only to ensure that time would not be wasted reading the proposal line by line, but also to make sure that our participants did not barter in public). It also clarified the focus of what we were trying to accomplish and fit the advice of a current principal of an experimental school who told me, "Don't try to do too much; do a few things well, and it will succeed." The research group distributed a research and collaborative experimentation matrix, which included a continuous evaluation component, course and degree offerings for school staff, grant-writing opportunities, research approval process, and training and coteaching opportunities. Governance did not fully articulate the relationship between the school and the university involvement, and, as I described earlier, that would provide the opening for a much more tangible joint proposal.

The curriculum area, because the Steering Committee members from DCPS were from the Office of Instructional Leadership, was very powerful in promoting not only their competency-based curriculum but also their configuration of providing services to students. The input from DCPS, above all the other sections of the drafts, was the most comprehensive here. When the university talked about inclusion and the servicing of exceptional education students in regular classrooms, DCPS objected. Other areas of contention would have to be worked out by the Steering Committee later.

Meanwhile, research completed their work and I sent them a note of things to consider, such as waivers needed for COE staff in the school and connection to specific projects—alternative assessment, time versus competency-based learning, alternative scheduling, teacher as researcher, adding philosophically a commitment to innovation and change, development and dissemination of innovations, the relationship to an advisory, and research funding. In order to guide a cohesive product, I suggested the following be addressed for the curriculum group: When and who will plan the integrated curriculum, and what other areas are impacted by the configuration? Inservicing of teachers must be planned up front in relation to funding. Assessment should be related to the competencies or some alternative means of evaluation. All the separate subject area plans must be interwoven into a scheme for curriculum that is student centered as suggested in the conceptualization of this section. Also, most of the real work was being done by one member from the COE and one person from DCPS. Neither side made contact beyond the required meeting except for these two. The idea was for each group to form a collaborative, and DCPS did not seem to be playing by those rules but by their own. Meetings were formal rather than informal, information disseminating rather than dialogue creating. Physical plant seemed to be focused on parking space, while school-based management and governance needed refocusing with a view toward collaborative governance.

To prepare for the next Steering Committee meeting at the end of April, 1993, our team members met and discussed progress to date. Some crucial conceptual ideas emerged from this meeting. We discussed the advisory for the school and the relationship of the university in this aspect. Ideas for full participation were that the composition be one person as the dean's appointment, three other faculty from the COE, one lay person, two parents, principal, lead teacher, and two other teachers. We would insist on a long term for the principal and that the advisory be empowered for decision making. The group also detailed a philosophy statement centered around a spirit of collegial governance with a commitment to innovation and change.

It is interesting that, after the subcommittee work was done, this would evolve as a major theme. What was the collaboration at this point, and what was the commitment on both sides? Our team was definitely concerned with encouraging and supporting the professional development of teachers, encouraging the use of research to improve classroom practice, and developing and disseminating effective innovative methods and materials tested through research.

Our people, particularly the group of untenured faculty participating in this project, were still wary that their efforts would not count toward tenure. They are correct, if the dean does not support innovation and change in concrete ways. When asked about faculty assignments and load being tied into the school project, the dean made evident that research and service were equated with participation.

The resultant statement taken to the Steering Committee meeting was as follows:

Philosophy/Mission Statement for Project Co-Staar

The Dade County Public School System and Florida International University present this proposal for the establishment of an elementary relief school on the University Park Campus. This school represents a spirit of collegial governance with a commitment to innovation and change. The aims of the collaboration are to encourage and support the professional development of teachers, encourage the use of research to improve classroom practice, and to develop and disseminate effective innovative methods and materials tested through research.

The Steering Committee reviewed the compilation of materials I prepared (a summary of all the group work to date). Their cochair from the curriculum committee handed out a revised version with more subject area sections. DCPS directed the meeting by having each subcommittee chair review his or her section. I thought this was perfunctory and repeatedly tried to direct the conversation to an analysis of the commonalities among all the materials, but we were on DCPS turf. Repeatedly when I tried to synthesize, they rushed us along and said that would be for the next time after everyone reviewed the written materials and used a "green pen to edit." We at the university use red pens, except for correcting the papers of our Taiwan students (red is not appropriate in their culture).

The site planning lease agreement was being worked out and the budget phase would follow, we were told by DCPS! Next time we would look at waivers, we were told! This was all rather presumptuous since the real work of synthesizing the recommendations of the subcommittees, a task I thought would be the province of the Steering Committee meeting, still had to be done. I also was sure that we were not in full agreement over the content. Some of the areas that were acceptable and expected by them were areas we had reservations about. So, I asked about a time line for completion of the proposal. The chair from DCPS steered us toward September, 1993, which, by the way, would postpone the school opening to 1996 or later! The time bomb exploded as DCPS wielded the political power and control. When was this decided? Did FIU/COE have a say in this? Is this why no real work was being done today? What control are they wielding that is directing this? Who had offended whom?

This was a formal meeting with a hurried tone. It was information giving—giving to FIU/COE. Why weren't we privy to the announcements? What had occurred to delay this project again? There were also aspects of the proposal in each area that were causing resistance. The governance group still was not decisive about the nature of the relationship of the participants from the university in the school-based management, shared decision-making structure, whether there could be a university liaison position on the cadre, or how the grade-level configuration would influence the structure of staffing. Other administrative issues were also placed on the table, such as the teachers writing the curriculum, and the use of an alternative calendar (this was receiving growing interest throughout the country, and I thought that DCPS would like a site to experiment with). This latter suggestion seemed an appropriate choice since we would be using the university facilities for the school, and the university calendar differed from that of Dade County. The logical alternative could be year-round school or extended day. Many of the ideas to be implemented successfully would need some coordinator to direct the flow of research, teacher training, in-service, and classes on site, and to ensure full participation of the COE staff members.

Another area that manifested itself by resistance to change was the mission statement we presented. Immediately the union representative said the union was not mentioned in the first sentence and that parents and community were not mentioned, whereupon my frustration at the whole tenor of the meeting came to a head. I felt that we were operating in ways that certainly did not match the whole point of the mission statement, which was collegial governance and change. The organizational influence and mode of operation of DCPS was very apparent in their machine-like implementation and microplanning. No one wanted to redirect their attention away from the details to conceptualize the big picture. I felt that DCPS's orders were to stall.

I wrote a memorandum to the dean expressing my concerns about the school. The endless delays up to now were only a prelude to the delays that would follow. Time became a crucial element in the wielding of power and influence. We wanted the process to move along. DCPS could wait and delay and build other schools until we either lost interest or the players whom they did not trust or want to participate moved on to other projects. It was suggested that we put limits on the lease agreement so that there would be a fail-safe date and that this might move them along. This was probably naive on our part since the more demands we made, the more rules and regulations they invoked to delay the process. Nonetheless, our administration needed to consider the following points:

1.   A change in the projected date of completion of the school from winter 1995, to the beginning of the school year 1996 at the earliest. This represented a one-and-a-half-year delay. Can we ensure that there will not be other postponements? Perhaps a time limit could be appended to the lease agreement.

2.   There is a core group of faculty now committed to working on this project long term. We believe that their involvement will be directed elsewhere if this project is unduly postponed. This also affects applications for grants to fund innovations and research proposal acceptance by permission givers. A meeting was set up with the provost, president, dean, and our cochairs.

As it turned out, something had happened. This school is less a College of Education school than a relief school based on an agreement between the president of the university and the superintendent. If it evolved into a collaboration, it would be an FIU and DCPS collaboration. Ultimatums were falling on deaf ears, so, if the president and superintendent wanted to continue, it would; if we want to push and make demands, they would stall and delay. They trust individuals, not the COE. The question was, did they trust me enough to be sure that I was negotiating in good faith. I had to make this apparent to the university administration without antagonizing my colleagues.

Was there a crisis? I wrote in my notes that I thought not. Symbolically having a building on site is important, but was it important to the COE or the university? I did not understand then that it was to the university. If they decided to stop the program, we could investigate other forms of funding and we could create a Developmental Research School like other sites in the state, but there would be no collaboration. And, it was the collaboration that I was after—with new ways to communicate, new ways to talk to each other, new avenues of support and cooperation.

Etzioni's (1993) communitarian agenda relates to the consequences of pulling out. First is a loss of trust; DCPS would never again enter into a bargaining arrangement with us. Second, a loss of participants' credibility, which now is pretty solid, especially since they feel we are being manipulated. Third, is a sense of enhancement of social cooperation and reduction of contentiousness. Fourth, turf wars cause harm to others, and I can't believe that it is DCPS's intention to harm the COE or to reaffirm our inability to work together. Fifth, a balance of the quest between institutions is really the quest among individuals, and progress has been made. Sixth, what we lose by succeeding in a power play is just not worth the trade-off in the long run. Lastly, bridging the gap between political theory and practice requires participatory democracy, as Dewey said. The participation creates a community that is freer, and, we were beginning to sense the importance of that freedom. That freedom was what I came to the university to participate in. It was something I had always felt was missing from the twenty-one years I had spent in the public school system. Maintenance is not freedom.

The May 1993 letter to the president outlined the following concerns:

1.   The projected date of completion of the school on campus was winter 1995. This date has been postponed by the DCPS until February 1996 at the earliest with a strong possibility of further delays.
2.   There is a core group of universitywide faculty now committed to working long term on this project. Their involvement will be directed elsewhere if this project is unduly postponed.
3.   The finished subcommittee work is now undergoing editing and will be ready for school board and university approval in September 1993.
4.   Could we proceed, keeping as close to the original date as possible, with the commitment of key College of Education staff to assist the process by working contiguously with DCPS to actualize the school?

5. The Board of Regents is aware of this project, and we can anticipate approval now. This may be uncertain if there are further delays.

6. Participation in this project spans all departments within the COE and involves professors in other colleges. Each participant worked cooperatively with his or her counterpart in the DCPS to actualize ideas and dreams into a finished proposal, which now is being edited by the Steering Committee.

At a meeting with the president, we discussed the issues of delay and maintaining interest of faculty, loss of trust, credibility on our part if we withdrew, enhanced social cooperation and reduced contentiousness, turf wars without harm to others, their intent in delay, and the balance between institutions and individuals. What would we lose by succeeding? Not as much as we could gain by moving on. The real partners in this agreement would now talk together and determine the fate of the project.

The June 1993, next meeting of the Steering Committee started with the announcement by DCPS that the lease agreement had been sent to FIU. They announced that the superintendent wanted to move ahead more quickly so the school could start and that this was now a priority. For the very first time, we knew what the announcements were before the meeting.

There also was now a plan for governance that was to change the nature of future negotiations and interactions between the players. DCPS proposed that we consider the Yale Child Study Program's COMER project for the school governance plan. DCPS had just sent a number of people for training, and conceptually it seemed to fit into our philosophy. Year-round school and a modified calendar were discussed, and a state-of-the-art technology emphasis, which would link the planned new COE building directly to the school, seemed a great idea. Phases of implementation in innovations needed to be addressed, but we left this meeting with a new sense that we were now dialoguing about macrodimensions that were vital to a collaboration and a governance structure that would include a member of the faculty in a collaborative decision-making role. I would be that faculty member.

I agreed that I would prepare a faculty involvement analysis for the proposal to describe what we would contribute to the school and that I would contact Yale to see if I could participate in the training for the following February.

A September 1993 correspondence from the COE to DCPS decries the number of critical initiatives supportive of each others' needs and aspirations and, even more importantly, the educational needs and aspirations of students in our public schools. These initiatives and collaborative undertakings range from the creation of a new elementary school on FIU's grounds to developing innovative curricula and research programs for emotionally disturbed middle-school students (Project United), to providing LEP children and their parents with specialized language programs (FELP), to Peace Corps volunteers for teaching careers in high-need curricular areas, to working with GMCC to develop, implement, and evaluate a districtwide mentoring and preventive juvenile delinquency program (Good Life). Also described were the Haitian assist children project (AMEN), the competency-based curriculum, and the participation of our dean and DCPS on the Florida Commission on Education Reform and Accountability. The competency-based curriculum was emerging as a model of locally-based results oriented public education. The end of the memorandum states that we stand on the threshold of giving new meaning to the term *partnership*.

My concern with all of these initiatives is that they are fleeting moments, marking a transitory coming together of participants for projects that are not sustainable and do not change the way each of us works culturally. Just letting it happen, as our dean suggested, is not enough to support sustainable innovations and certainly not to sustain collaborations. It is too easy to complete a project and terminate any cooperative work. Then we are back to the normal mode of operation of each organization, and failure to sustain is housed in blame that the other side did not contribute what they said they would in terms of resources, both personnel and funds. This change in perspective to transform somehow this opportunity into a true collaboration was the next phase of the process, and it meant that resistance had to be overcome on both sides, leverage and power wielding had to be diminished, and each organization had to be a willing learning organization that was open to innovations and new ways of interfacing.

Chapter Six
Resistance, Leverage, and Learning Organizations

I was watching *Firing Line* one Saturday morning in April 1993, as William F. Buckley was orchestrating a discussion concerning whether women in the military should engage in combat. He made the statement, "Sometimes resistance to change is for a good reason." We tend to focus, especially when trying to create something new and innovative, on the change itself. But, change is a gradual process. It takes part of the past with it in the formation of the new. The wealth of writing based on paradigm shifts (Kuhn, 1970) offers a clear explanation. Acceptance of new theories in science is gradual, and changes in belief systems are at the heart of the transition. When organizations resist change, their resistance is based on the beliefs and understandings of the present. For DCPS, resistance to outside influences and shifts in operation are due to the maintenance of the system, the perpetuation of lines of authority, a belief that the modes of behavior are correct, and a distrust of anything new to accomplish the objectives and goals of the organization. Compounding this resistant stance is a history of failures in the past and of unreliability of follow-through in others who are not under their authority.

Culture changes that challenge and reform belief systems are difficult to enact, but facilitation and development of new identities are possible between people (Frost et al., 1991, 298). Argyris (1990, 6–9) warned that care must be taken not to confound errors of perception through actions that are intended to increase understanding and trust but produce just the opposite. Don't blame others or the system for poor decision making. Don't let the tradition dominate organizational life. Allow for upward communication and input for difficult issues. Don't expect reason to dominate action, even when it is in the best interest of the players.

Argyris (1990, 100) provided a means of analysis of the effects of governing conditions and organizational decision making. The organizational action map first describes the issue, problem, or situation along with the norms of organizational operation that impact on the issue. Second, action strategies are proposed. Then, consequences of each action are taken to three levels of consequences so that each consequence is fully explored and solutions are not undermined. Finally, feedback to the governing conditions is provided so that policy can be altered to be reflective of input from all levels of the organization. It becomes even more important to play out the organizational decision making when two organizations are involved and their organizational maps align in different ways. Altering of governing conditions and jointly held consequences is an important part of the process of collaboration.

Overcoming resistance to change involves action strategies that are cognizant of the consequences that themselves result in consequences. Burns (1978, 417) described the strategies as coercive, normative, utilitarian, empirical rational, and reeducative. Coercive strategies involve the wielding of power and authority. Normative strategies involve the internalization of values that impact on behavior. Utilitarian strategies control the handing out or withholding of rewards and punishments to control behavior. Empirical rational strategies apply moral, economic, and political reasoning to achieve change. Reeducative strategies exert influence through changes in feelings and thought.

My notes on the beginning of the 1993–1994 academic year document not only resistance to change, but also themes that began to emerge reflecting more resistance than collaboration. These themes can be exemplified by the following: "I don't want to play anymore and I'm taking my toys home"; "I want to change the rules"; "Let's play by my rules, not yours"; "Let's shift the burden of the work instead of sharing the responsibility," thus redirecting the blame. For FIU and the COE, each of these was manifested in a particular way. Withdrawing, as described previously, was our administrative response every time things did not seem to be going our way, or

DCPS flexed their muscles. Instead of withdrawing, DCPS used the strategy of delay, which worked well for them since their time line was not ours, and they could easily direct their focus elsewhere within the system or to other outside organizations that were more compliant than we were. When we tried to change the rules, they presented us with the union, the laws, or the rules and regulations they lived by, which helped them to function effectively and which we wanted to alter or change completely. Shifting the burden of work was an interesting phenomenon different from placing the blame. Within their organization, they had multiple participants, who duplicated expertise so they could pull someone off task and substitute another person who had no prior knowledge or commitment to the process, which already had been going on for some time. We, then, would have to work with another person as counterpart and "start over from scratch" each time.

By the summer of 1993, all the parts of the proposal had to be put together into a comprehensive meaningful whole. Four members of the Steering Committee accomplished only the initial editing of the proposal at a cut-and-paste session with the realization that some elements of the subcommittee work were not compatible or needed further explanation to be included in the final proposal. We were also asked by DCPS to clarify our commitment to the project by describing the scope of our involvement in the school so that it could be included in the proposal. I suspect they wanted a written commitment on our part that would explicitly delineate what we intended so they could communicate this to the School Board. The addition of the FIU contribution to the project was written by me and inserted into the proposal. It represents the essence of how we see our continued role and ongoing commitment to the school. The elements of this commitment were as follows:

FIU Statement of Contributory Effort to Implementation of Project Co-STAAR Philosophy/Mission Statement

The Dade County Public School System, Florida International University, and the United Teachers of Dade have collaborated toward the establishment of an elementary relief school on the University Park Cam-

pus. The school represents a spirit of collegial governance with a commitment to innovation and change. The aims of the collaboration are to encourage and support the professional development of teachers, encourage the use of research to improve classroom practice, and to develop and disseminate effective innovative methods and materials tested through research.

Florida International University faculty are committed to forming and maintaining a positive presence with school staff, administration, and the community of the school. As such, Florida International University and the College of Education will participate by providing expertise and resources in the following areas:

1.   Participation on an ongoing basis in the planning and coordinating of school activities as a voting member of the School Planning Management Team, and on subcommittees for research and experimentation, curriculum, community and parent linkages, and mental health (re: School Development Program Model). The goal of this interaction is consensual decision making through collaboration.

2.   Provide micro- and macrolevel planning assistance and expertise in formative assessment of achievement of program, student, institutional, and community goals while participating in systematic evaluation of the Comprehensive School Plan.

3.   Provide for staff development needs:

> *a. related to short- and long-term needs; b. pre-opening for induction, training, and orientation; c. through in-service training; d. through graduate-level courses leading toward advanced degrees at the Master's, Specialist, and Doctoral levels; e. recertification coursework; f. as evolving through the Comprehensive School Plan.*

4.   Participate in selection of principal and staff through involvement in the DCPS/FIU/UTD established selection process.

5.   Provide assessment and validation analyses and dissemination of:

> *a. program by critically identifying successful and innovative teaching methodologies; b. student achievement; c. curriculum modification; d. alternative assessment; e. instructional materials and techniques.*

6. *Provide faculty with technical and practical support through:*

    a. classroom research dissemination; b. modeling; c. demonstration; d. participatory planning.

7. *Provide resources and expertise through the Florida International University community for family services as appropriate to identified needs and interests and to pursue grants and outside funding as needs are made apparent.*

8. *Florida International University will provide:*

    a. undergraduate pre-service interns and field placements on a continual basis in order to supplement the adult/student ratio within classrooms; b. tutoring services; c. library access for staff; d. family workshops and lectures; e. faculty member to act as liaison between the school and the College of Education for coordination of research, placement of interns, and participation on the school-based management team (jointly selected by DCPS/FIU/UTD); f. a recreation, sports, and movement activity program through the Health, Physical Education and Recreation Department.

    Florida International University supports the Yale Child Study Center School Development Program as a model of consensual decision making and collaboration to guide the governance of the school. A staff member will work cooperatively with DCPS/UTD and receive advanced training in this model.

    FIU is committed to this COMER Model because it exemplifies the spirit of community that prompted the initiation of this venture originally. Involvement of parents, mental health members, and the School Planning Management Team are the mechanisms that will flow into a dynamic Comprehensive School Plan that is supported by staff development that is relevant, appropriate, and responsive to authentic assessment that produces quality.

    Since the participating organizations are charting new ground through this collaborative effort, FIU recognizes that our commitment to an active presence with the school and staff is paramount. We project that this model of interaction will lead to the establishment of a center for research and dissemination of innovative practice that can serve the needs of South Florida and the entire southeast region. FIU staff will

INTERACTIVE MODEL

FIU	ACTION RESEARCH PROJECTS → ←	Project Co-STAAR SPMT	COLLABORATIVE PROJECTS → ←	DCPS
• Department Input • Contracts and Grants				• Office of Instructional Leadership • Contracts/Grants

• Coursework
• Individual Research Agenda (streamlined process)
• Innovative Programs (contracts and grants)
• Training
• Evaluation (formative and summative)
• Dissemination of Research

• Action Research Committee
• Inputs to School Planning Management Team
• Co-Chaired: DCPS/FIU
• Other Interested Teachers, University Faculty
• Relevant DCPS/University Administrators

• Coursework/Workshops
• Institutional Research Agenda (streamlined research process)
• Development of Curriculum and Instruction Dissemination to Other Sites
• Ongoing Evaluation (formative and summative)
• Dissemination of Research and Practice

offer specialized training and support of "cutting-edge" innovative pro-grams as identified by the School Planning Management Team and of-fer further dissemination of practice contractually requested by DCPS.

As part of the collaborative effort between DCPS/UTD/FIU, the following represent the research goals. To:

• promote collaboration between institutions of higher learning and state educational systems including practitioners and administrators;
• provide leadership in the identification of educational needs and prob-lems;
• provide leadership in the identification of new knowledge about teach-ing and learning;
• provide leadership in the translation of new knowledge into class-room practice;
• provide leadership in the evaluation of new classroom practices; and
• provide leadership in the dissemination of research findings and in-structional materials.

The model on the previous page illustrates the interactive nature of the action research collaboration, which will be implemented at Project Co-STAAR.

Other than this addition, there was a decided lack of progress over the summer. By August, my notes describe my trepidation and feeling that DCPS was pulling back from true involvement and that something extraordinary needed to happen to regain their trust and move the project forward. This movement would have to be in a way that was not directed by permission givers but had a life of its own through the people who participated and who had a stake in the future of the project. Success then would be personal positives, and meaningfulness of involvement would be the symbol of progress.

The previous June, the Steering Committee had decided to meet on August 9, 1993. I showed up at the DCPS office and went up-stairs to the meeting. This was to be with the eight members of the Steering Committee working together to edit the first full draft of the proposal. They forgot; some were on vacation; only one other member of the COE team showed up; the missing piece on demo-graphics of the community was not done by the DCPS side. I asked that they reschedule the meeting, and, as it turned out, the symbols of power and authority prevailed as they called the dean's office to establish the date. No apology, no excuses, it just occurred. We had grown apart, and something needed to be done to bring us together again.

This atmosphere persisted at the rescheduled meeting in September 1993. We met at the DCPS office. This always was a more formal affair than when we met at FIU. The union representative was there, and evidently this was the first time he saw the draft. He complained that he was being left out of the information loop and requested that all materials be circulated through him. Why this was not done by DCPS I do not know, but he assumed it was FIU that was being noncommunicative. Another barrier to trust was erected.

The four representatives from FIU sat throughout this meeting while the DCPS people came in and went out. The DCPS chair had complaints, one being that FIU had not responded to the site planning document sent to them last April. Since the DCPS chair now was in charge of the proposals for innovative schools, he wanted us to complete the proposal to go to the Board by February when two other proposals would be on the School Board's agenda. He questioned whether people from the president's office had visited prototype schools in the area as intended. This is an interesting point since the Steering Committee had long ago abandoned the notion of designing a new school building in favor of adapting a prototype to our needs, which was more economical. He left the room after the announcements and another member of the Steering Committee came in and basically talked about the Competency Based Curriculum, which we had already agreed to incorporate into the proposal. Time, by withholding it for productive work, manifests itself as a barrier supportive of resistance to change. They also presented us with a new format for the proposal that was really not any different from the old, but this too used up valuable time. The purpose of the meeting was to do joint editing; we did everything but that.

Additional information given by DCPS people described some coventure legal questions (something the lawyers had to iron out), waiver requests needing to be charted out after the proposal was complete, a time line after going to the board of eighteen months (which would make opening after February of 1995), and the feeling that the burden to move along was on FIU shoulders. Was the delay now on our part? Were they merely reacting to perceived resistance from us to move along? That certainly was not how our participants felt. We were willing and eager to complete the proposal, but instead we talked endlessly about aspects over which we had no control.

Something extraordinary had to move this process along. Something that would reestablish trust and collaboration to work out the differences and resistance exhibited at the last meeting was necessary. I had been tentatively accepted into the COMER training at Yale and only needed a letter from DCPS requesting that I be included in their training contract. After securing funds through a grant to pay for my training week, I wrote out a note for DCPS to send supporting my participation and gave it to them at the end of this meeting. I was hoping that a week spent in a different environment would give Steering Committee participants (two from their side and myself) the opportunity to move the project forward.

On Saturday, February 12, 1994, I left for Yale. The worst storm of the year in the Northeast broke just enough for me to fly to New Haven, Connecticut, to participate in the School Development Program facilitator's training. I took an earlier flight than the rest of the Dade County people. Two of the seven DCPS people being trained are also on the Steering Committee for the project.

In any change effort there is the possibility that the intent of the restructuring effort will be transformed when in practice over a period of time. That was also a possibility in this project. Allowing and supporting my participation in the COMER training ensures that FIU/COE personnel will participate ongoing in the school at a level where our input will not be seen as imposition or dictating of a position that is not in congruence with that of DCPS. DCPS sent the letter to Yale asking that I be included in this advanced training and thereby enhanced the mutual commitment to a process designed to facilitate collaboration. I reviewed the first week of training; viewed all the tapes and went over the facilitator training workshop they participated in last year. My notes on that week describe my optimism: "So, I sit here with nineteen inches of snow outside awaiting their flight later in the day. I look out the window. It is clear and bright, cold and refreshing. Will the school be that? Can we make something unique happen? Something good that everyone is proud of without the game playing and finger pointing?"

The School Development Program started in 1968 as a collaboration between the Yale Child Study Center and the public school system in New Haven, Connecticut. It is based on the theory that children develop along six pathways: physical, cognitive, psychological/emotional, speech and language, social interactive, and moral. The resultant School Development Program, or the COMER process, has nine components. There are three mechanisms for implementing change. They consist of the school planning and management team, the mental health or student services team, and a comprehensive participatory parent's program. The vehicles for operating each of these mechanisms are through a comprehensive school plan jointly developed, modified, documented, and evaluated; a staff development program; and continuous assessment and modification. The three guidelines that permeate the mechanisms and operations are "no fault" or no blame allowed, "consensual decision making," and "collaboration." These nine elements form the basis for changing the organization and operation of a school, a process through which shared governance and collaboration through participation is a reality. Clearly these elements are the same as those being sought by the collaboration: to design the school on campus, and thus, provide a process by which we can collaboratively participate equally in the decision making of the school once it is built.

To prepare for the week of training I had to fill out an *Attitude Skills and Knowledge Inventory* and an *Implementation Perception Survey*. Some of the questions proved valuable to my analysis of the school project, and I set about answering them from that perspective. By reflecting on them, I hoped to understand how the progress of the Steering Group could be moved along within a spirit of cooperation. What follows are selected answers I gave to the questions.

What has hindered most the successful implementation in your district? For the district in which the university is located, implementation can be directed from the school district level and restrictions also have central control. Loosening of these rules could contribute to more successful dissemination as well as implementation.

In your view, how does the school and classroom organization affect student learning and development? Both school and classroom reflect organizational culture—the rules, roles, and responsibilities as well as possibilities in staff and students. An atmosphere that is positive, success oriented, and collaborative fosters student learning and growth. The entire community contributes to this.

In your current situation, what steps can be taken to provide optimal conditions for student learning and development? For the university to not dictate but to be aware of the realities of the school district and the pressures they are under from the public.

As a COMER facilitator, how do you feel you would be able to foster these conditions? Participatory representation of the university/college I work in is important in establishing trust for collaborative efforts.

What are your views on school change? The rhetoric on systemic change lately seems to be talk of power and empowerment—change for change's sake. I believe in planned change that evolves, taking with it elements of the old. Reformers must ask, "What is happening that is relevant and successful for the humanistic enterprise we are engaged in?" Then ask, "How can we plan together for the future so that all stakeholders can balance competition for resources and time?"

What have you found to be the most effective strategies for monitoring implementation of the program in your district? Situational analysis; indicators of involvement by all concerned groups; student motivation; teacher efficacy indicators.

What strategies do you use to evaluate the impact of your current school change effort? As appropriate, use of formative evaluation, contextual analysis, programmatic evaluation at the micro and macrolevel, and process and product analysis. The indicators of successful programmatic change must be broader than achievement and standardized scores.

Which of those strategies do you find most useful? Continuous collaboration analysis monitored by keeping the information flow as open as possible and keeping it out on the table as honestly as possible.

What is your view of collaborative school management? Collaborative school governance is a better term. Management infers a factory model.

Collaboration is hard enough! I do not feel the current movement in professionalization of teachers will be successful if management functions are the goal. To me, collaboration is a collective trusting environment where the goals/objectives of a site are determined, refined, implemented, and evaluated thoughtfully, honestly, and without undue restrictions on time and personnel.

Please identify some of the barriers to parent involvement and the strategies you used to try to overcome them. Barriers: Time, information, expectations, and past experience with limited accessibility; overwhelmed with the organization and structure of school. Strategies: Make site inviting, informative, accessible—open to parent needs as well as student needs.

In what ways do you think schools are similar to other organizations, and in what ways are schools unique? Schools are similar in organization to businesses; principals are trained in management techniques fueled by accountability and efficiency. Only lately has this factory metaphor changed; and rightly so, students are again being looked at as unique individuals. Governance of school districts remains and maintains this management perspective and bureaucratic structure. This is hard to overcome. The pendulum shift has to move away from standardization; each school community must create and sustain a culture of its own.

In what ways has your understanding of schools as organizations helped in facilitating change in the schools in your district? For the university/school project I am involved in, the two organizations have vastly different operating structures, and the collaboration of building, running, and sustaining an innovative school on our campus has required a hybrid organizational model to be successful.

How would you go about training the staff on key organizational management and behavior concepts? Facilitate discussion using situational analysis of real-life on-site issues relevant to the staff. Create an atmosphere that supports problem-solving behaviors that are nonthreatening, nonpunitive.

Characteristics of a supportive climate? Nonthreatening, nonpunitive, creative, eclectic, synergistic, high productivity, high energy, innovation from bottom-up, success-oriented, high efficacy in staff and students.

What is your view on the idea that the change is an essential aspect of individual and collective growth in schools? Planned change promotes growth by taking what is and adapting to forces, internal and external, that are part of evolution. By anticipating the future, it is more controllable; planners and participants can foresee what changes are necessary to fully participate in the future. Change means choices, opportunities for growth.

Discuss how you have prepared staff in your district for implementing a program of change and how you have helped to facilitate that change process. At the university we try to instill in students the opportunity to create change when they go to work for school districts. Staff in the districts for which they work show much resistance to change. They are bombarded with innovation and new programs constantly and become satiated with reform efforts and are less participatory than the numbers of innovations would suggest.

What are the stages and key elements of change? Resistance, reeducation/buy-in, adoption as own, innovation personalized.

How important do you think it is for a leader to be a good listener? Very. A good leader knows what their followers need, want, and what of the leader's expectations could be realized. This is accomplished metaphorically by listening and by walking around, by letting followers know the leader is authentic, trusting, and consistent.

How important do you think it is for leader to be facilitator? Leaders must lead; facilitators often cannot allow their own expectations to interfere with the group process. Therefore, facilitators must allow the process of give-and-take and decision making to occur from within the group. This often is harder than being a leader.

It is Sunday, and the DCPS group apparently reached New Haven in the middle of the night but their luggage didn't. We were all on unfamiliar turf. Coupled with winter problems, which we do not face in Florida, this made for camaraderie. I had a connection with the two participants on the Steering Committee. The COMER process creates an atmosphere conducive to cooperative, collaborative sharing that I hoped would permeate the week and influence our progress at home. The purpose of the COMER training is to facilitate the creation of a shared community, which then could be replicated situationally at sites selected for implementation in the participants' own school districts.

I was placed on a team with one of my fellow Steering Committee members. In the course of the day, we decided to meet for dinner to talk about the progress of the group and to work out the remaining details. We had authority to do this since I was cochair of our team members, and she was responsible on the DCPS side for the proposal preparation. I was told that the proposal was being formatted into acceptable form. I noted that I was concerned that there was a holdup, and that it might be on our end.

The COMER program creates a very positive atmosphere, one that the facilitators hope will be duplicated at the sites of implementation. The nature of the COMER model makes it so. This program of participatory decision making for a school definitely matched the conceptual nature of our proposed elementary school and could provide the missing link in the school governance part of the proposal.

Being on the same team as the DCPS Steering Committee member was not an accident. The facilitators understood why I was there (I had spoken to them prior to the training), and grouping us together was an example of putting their program into action. It seemed to be working out very well. I talked to one of the Yale facilitators responsible for university linkages, and he told me about how university partnerships work re the COMER model. Universities remit a fee to the Yale Child Study Center to be a partner and to receive technical support. Then the university provides support to the school system. I mentioned this to the DCPS person, and she said that would be wonderful; then DCPS could facilitate through FIU and utilize the College of Education as a training site. I hoped that throughout the week we could work out any differences in process to get the school project completed.

What is unique about COMER? It is a process. I have some real reservations about the implementation re curriculum and instruction. At that stage, COMER sometimes becomes aligned with product and the controversy of product assessment. If conception of curriculum is very narrow, instructional implementation is not congruent with COMER's process-oriented goals. But, taken as a process for facilitation of a community committed to students and school, COMER is both conceptually and in practice very successful.

The next day I was invited to accompany the DCPS people to a lunch meeting with their assigned facilitator. The facilitators are planning a visit in April to do training with the principals and school-based management teams of the thirteen existing COMER schools in DCPS. They needed a place to meet in April, so I offered the university if it could be arranged. The DCPS people liked that. I suggested that we, then, at some later point if there was interest by faculty, participate more fully in the process of training and facilitation of the school on campus and of the training in the existing sites. They liked that, too. I suggested that we at the university meet with the COMER facilitator while he was in Miami about involving the COE in the process in Dade. He said that would be fine.

Did either of us have any power to make these overtures to COMER? I did, since the nature of my involvement was to be trained to ultimately be the facilitator of the school and participate fully as ongoing representative of the COE. The DCPS people, on the other hand, clearly were in line positions and could not commit to anything or make independent decisions without checking the hierarchy of permission givers. Power, remember, lies in position and title for DCPS. So, even if we talked about creating linkages, those linkages had to be formally established and understood by the hierarchy. Then there was the risk of interpretation since, for each organization, we assume that we speak the same language and therefore have common meaning and purpose. One of the COMER facilitators calls this displacement. What is displaced is the word, not the concept or idea. We just have different words to describe the same thing, and if the goals are similar, the words become inconsequential to the actions.

On the whole, this was a successful trip. Whatever clouded the atmosphere of the last Steering Committee meeting and created an overtly resistant stance on the part of the DCPS people was not present here at all. Some personal relationships were established, but more importantly, the university now had a presence in an important initiative for innovation and change.

By March of 1994 I knew that their impatience had to do with the legal document for the land lease still sitting on our administration's desk after three months. (It finally was sent to DCPS in April.) It had to do with, in their view, vacillation and rehashing of nonnegotiable points by people external to the Steering Committee. Meanwhile, the Steering Committee members on our side functioned without benefit of knowledge, the same knowledge that was not withheld from DCPS. Our lack is the result of not having a vehicle of current information sharing other than by word of mouth. DCPS lines of communication are clear, memo-driven pronouncements of policy. Ours are in the field and based on practice. Each individual guards and shares with no one because our side doesn't recognize the value and validity of the memo-driven lines of communication.

Ancillary to the school project, I was on the lookout for programs that could conceptually be placed in the school to further enhance the relationship between the COE and DCPS. One such program was Reading Recovery, and the possibility of training one of our staff members to provide certified Reading Recovery teacher training using the school facility as home base was moving through the permission givers of the university. More importantly, this was a program that DCPS wanted, and, with one of our staff members, I figured out a way to make this a reality. Of course, I was not a member of elementary education and was developing this initiative only out of my involvement with the development of the school project. Reading Recovery would require office space, two-way mirrors, and a liaison between the university and the students/staff of the school district. The consent to proceed with the feasibility of this project was given by the dean's office, and elementary education was now questioning why they were not asked to participate in the decision to proceed. It is interesting that an individual may act as an entrepreneur at the university as long as he or she does not step over the boundaries of another person's perceived sphere of interest. (Notice that I did not say influence since that would require praxis!) Since I am not aligned to a specific subject area, my development work is largely conceptual in nature and I try to create linkages. It is my belief that at the university you do not sit in judgment about the actions taken by other members of the community when the decision to be involved is an open process, especially if you choose not to act. If that action takes the form of building walls and instituting impediments to progress, then that is not community building, collegial, or an exercise of freedom, which is the nature of university work.

Therefore, we went ahead in May with the proposal and went to share it with the administration of DCPS; the same players as the Steering Committee cochairs with the addition of the dean for budget and finance; and the person willing to leave home and hearth for New Zealand for a year of training. The meeting with DCPS went well. They suggested that our relationship for training be for three years and that a memorandum be presented to the School Board in July so that they knew of our intent.

The School Board of Dade County, that July, listened to the presentation by the dean on the benefits of adding Reading Recovery to the twelve collaborations that were already under way with the COE. One board member brought up a concern about commitment on the part of the teachers they would send to the university for training. This was interesting as the dialogue paralleled the discussion we had had about sending someone at our expense for a year of training and asking them for a commitment to stay with the university for a specified period of time. Made public and for the record by the dean was that this was part of an outgrowth of negotiations for the elementary school on campus. The associate superintendent for instruction made it a point to formally introduce me and the person who would be trained from our staff, and the superintendent expressed his hopes that we would be back soon for approval of the proposal for the school on campus. He used the word *collaboration*!

Where was the collaboration? When I left for a vacation, I knew the lease agreement in final form would be ready soon. I knew that the final proposal needed work, but a large portion of the remaining editing and omissions had to come from DCPS people. At that point, there had been no changes made since the last editing on disk by myself. A large part of that editing had been the inclusion of the commitment FIU would make to the school, which was further expanded by my being trained to be the school site COMER facilitator.

Meanwhile, DCPS principals already involved in COMER who attended the training that we sponsored in Miami were starting to ask about the school. They requested that we come out and meet with them to see what they are doing at their sites. Being assigned to a new school is a plus, but working with an innovation such as our collaborative venture seemed to be generating a lot of interest. DCPS also has asked me to participate in negotiations they were having concerning a proposal for the establishment of a master's program in urban education. Did they now view me as a mediator or translator of their wants, needs, and desires and ours? Was this a measure of success? The real test would be if we now could speed up the process and conclude the negotiations for the proposal. It would be symbolic for both organizations and provide the metaphor for the initiation of other programs that linked us in collaborative endeavors.

Chapter Seven
Organizational Systematics: A Virtual World

I attempted to finish this book while vacationing in Maine. The beauty of the beaches and lighthouses and the coolness of the weather provided a refreshing break from summer in Florida. Friends met us, and we stayed in a rented house for the week. Ed Brothers, a marine biologist trained at Scripps, asked me one day if I was familiar with the name Karl Popper. Popper participated in the discussions of the Vienna Circle, the analytic philosophers who promoted logical positivism and scientific proof through meaning to produce certainty. Popper recognized a fallacy in this approach since there is a limitation to the amount of data that can be collected to support a hypothesis. Never could the universe of support be gathered, and one conflicting piece of data can destroy the hypothesis completely. Rather than look for supporting data, look instead, Popper suggested, for the fallacies. The theory that cannot be falsified is the theory that is acceptable. Scientists, then, who look for support for their theory, create a pseudoscience, in which the original hypothesis is self-corroborated and all detractors to the theory are not even considered.

Brothers went on to describe how there has been a philosophical shift in science, particularly as it relates to evolution of species, from the linear lines of ancestry to phylogenetic systematics. This new point of view relates to Popper's falsifications and is the link to the shift toward Kuhnian scientific revolutions. Kuhn (1970) argued that science progresses within a structure of presuppositions that directs methodology. To change paradigms requires a conceptual shift of intellectual angst. The positions representing the old and new are not rational extensions but emotional irrationalities bound by group affiliation and majority rule. The community of scientists makes the rules for their corner of the world, just as in this study, each organization creates its own emotional standards and collective assent. The new requires that allegiance be transferred from one paradigm to the other, and this cannot be done with power, influence, or coercion.

Popper's influence, then, implies that we observe from a particular point in time and utilize our skills, techniques, and methodologies to create theories. Because we are part of the process, participating from a singular point in the continuum of time, we only view what is around us from the perspective of our particular scientific methodology. We try to create meaning and linkages by supporting that theory rather than allowing uncertainty and doubt to direct our exploration. We chart our course, make our maps, and organize the world around our perspective, which may be false. This is what happens in closed systems based on traditional assumptions. Time is the crucial element. We exist in one time frame, or within one organization, and only look at the world from that vantage point. For an observer, like myself, who is not separate from the experiment, the quest for linkages is not always known because of the space and time the observer inhabits (Casti, 1989).

Phylogenetic systematics postulate that we should look to the characteristics that are apparent in species for their evolutionary linkages, not in presuppositions about where connections should be that are based on hypotheses, which may be false. Since we only view time from our vantage point and cannot, in our lifetime, hope to collect all the clues necessary to create all the linkages to eliminate doubt of lineage, let us then use what we do know to understand the inconsistencies that are the real clues to a much larger puzzle than we supposed.

How you look, within whatever time frame you inhabit, is based also on the tacit beliefs held by the observer. If we were all realists, interpretation would suppose that there is an objective reality that describes the world. Truth or falsity would be based on the accumulation of support for a theory, and overwhelming evidence of the majority would be the proof. Instrumentalists view methodology as the instrument for collection of evidence. Methodology provides the tools to predict the results of data collection and has no truth in and of itself. Relativism, though, suggests that the theory serves the purposes of the researcher and allows the theory to change over and over again as needed. It allows truth to be embedded in a time frame, recognizing that the moment we collect data or view an event what we get is only a partial picture from which to operate. Knowledge, facts, laws, and theories are relative to time, place, circumstance, and the recorder of truth. Therefore, knowledge changes, as it should, and old methods have to be revised because their surety and preciseness longitudinally can never be certain (Casti, 1989, 24–26).

Truth then is that which is supported by a specific set of data, and there may exist at the same time parallel truths and parallel knowledge. This study is relativistic and without the rationality and objectivity of pure science. There exists, for each revelation and conclusion I have drawn, a counterpoint that could be presented as equally viable. But, I did not create the reality; I only sought to describe it for understanding. Reality is what the community believes and states it operates under. Reality is also reflective of the habitus of community expectations and reproduction of belief. Looking at events in ways that challenge that belief and the underlying assumptions that produced it threatens the social order of the commonplace of assumptions we have about the way people live and work together. The social activity of investigation and experimentation is determined by the norms of that community. Innovation and solution finding require deviance from the accepted habitus of belief.

This case study is the systematic search for a language of conversation of the conditions that create a collaboration. The results and conclusions are drawn from observable data, filtered through the sensibilities of a discipline of training that I represent. The transferability and lessons to be learned are those of this project or of the establishment of a community; this community must be sensitive to looking beyond the realist and instrumental interpretations that often guide its actions. This study is an attempt to move toward the relativistic understanding that the new can happen in our time frame if we know how to look.

Thus, this analysis of a process leading toward collaboration is a situational analysis embedded in a particular time frame. It recognizes that all organizations are composed of a technical system that is formal, rule driven, and positivistic. The other competing system is a social system of informal groups and patterns of interaction, which are nested in the environment. An intervention or change in structure of an organization can be first order, which maintains the characteristics of the organization, or it can be second order, effecting the very character of the system (Bushe and Shani, 1991, 2, 3).

The systems investigated here are largely bureaucratic and have centralized control, task specialization and accountability, functional grouping, and internal standardization. These are strengths in dealing with the outside world, but when taken to excess become weaknesses of too much centralization. This results in problems with learning and adapting as central control decision makers don't hear or attend to important information. Knowledge becomes compartmentalized and withheld, it becomes functionally hard to process and gather, and it is hard to overcome the rules that are standardized and based on the history of the organization (Bushe and Shani,1991, 5–9).

What I have sought to document here is the emergence of a transorganizational alliance that transcends these limitations. Bushe and Shani (1991, 9–10) called these new formations parallel learning structures. They are created structures that operate alongside the formal hierarchy for the purpose of increasing learning in the organization. They infuse new behaviors and beliefs. These structures create the opportunity for thinking, talking, and acting differently because different norms and procedures evolve and promote learning. This theory of sociotechnical systems jointly optimizes through encouraging innovation rather than preservation, and enables the organization to develop human resources, cooperative efforts, commitment, energy, and social and technical resource use. It actually redesigns the process (Bushe and Shani, 1991, 159–160). That kind of change is what I believe came about through this project. The result is that we learn about them, they learn about us, and we each go back to our own organizations with new perspectives of how we can together accomplish those goals we have in common.

This organizational learning occurs by clarifying expectations so that they are achievable and visionable. Learning helps generate an accurate information flow so that distortion is reduced. Learning provides feedback loops used to break down boundaries between organizations. Learning allows us to share different points of view, to share different perspectives. Learning gives us the time to develop common perspectives, even when we run over schedule. Learning makes the future easier if we can protect the innovation from pressure for quick successes or threats of elimination (Bushe and Shani, 1991, 140–146).

Senge (1990) called this *ensemble development.* I think this term is very appropriate for this project. There has been assembled a cast of players—a traveling troupe of actors—who together have tried to build a structure with an enhanced capacity to achieve ambitious goals. It is an ensemble that does not merely duplicate performance from previous encounters but also creates new characterizations as it emerges. There occurred what Senge called (7) *systems thinking,* not just an accumulation of individual parts. Since interrelationships take years to play out the effects on each other, focusing on part of the system or on the artifacts of negotiations makes seeing patterns difficult. What is missed is an underlying worldview of the continuums of internal to external and formal to informal connections, which are sustainable long after the project is over. The structural maintenance of looking to each other for solutions to emergent problems, and the synergy of collective opportunities for integrating operations and for thinking and acting like a community are the signs that collaboration is a reality.

The real effects are in the mental models (Senge, 1990, 8) and images of assumptions, generalizations, and operation each organization has about the other. Team learning requires a synergy that begins with dialogue, thinking together, and overcoming patterns that undermine learning (Senge, 1990, 10). Actions and changes in structures lead to significant enduring improvements, but these require a commitment to the truth (Senge, 1990, 159).

The following diagram tries to operationalize this transition from individual organizations working in parallel to organizations that have learned to integrate operations and transformed their life of work into community-oriented collaborations. Figure 5, Zones of Organizational Involvement, visualizes three areas, or zones of influence. Zone I depicts the separate structures of each organization, each with its own tasks, charges, concerns, and way of operating. At the first level of interacting, each organization sends representatives to work together on a project. The underlying habitus is that individuals maintain the parent organization behaviors that are charac-

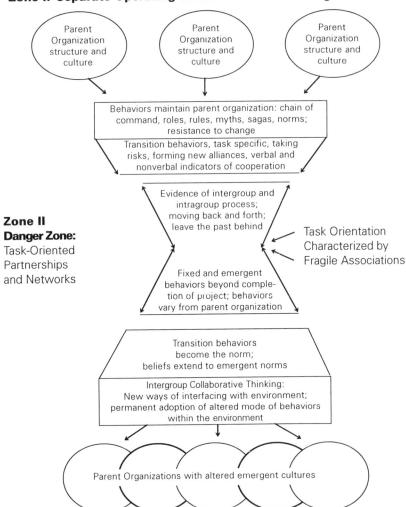

FIGURE 5   Zones of Organizational Involvement

teristic of their understanding of work. Cultural maintenance is primary. Resistance to change and cultural norms are adhered to. If this interaction persists, over time a second level of interaction occurs, and there appear to be transition behaviors that are task specific but require interactions that diverge from those of the parent organization to come into play to get the task or job done. Here participants take risks, form new alliances with persons from the other parent organizations, and make formal and informal connections that indicate movement toward the transorganizational behaviors described in Chapter 2.

Zone II shows the danger zone in which task orientation is toward completion of the project. Here, intergroup and intragroup processes are emerging in ways that clearly depart operationally from those of the parent organization, but this behavior requires a leap over a divide, which is experienced as a gorge with no safety net. Above the danger zone is an area where individuals move back and forth between their traditional way of working and thinking and the emergent mixture of new ways to work together. Below the danger zone are the partnerships and networks that begin to establish their own legitimacy of emergent behaviors to be responsive to each new task. This is a virtual structure at this point since it is not perceived by the outside world as fully formed. Each parent organization still has expectations for their workers but tradition is being altered by successful new ways of working that are impacting on the beliefs of the individuals involved. Of course, this is always in motion, moving toward Zone III and moving back toward Zone I. A state of flux that is not firmly part of the identity of the culture is characteristic of the collaborative that this structure could become.

Zone III is the collaboration area. It has two stages. The first is the transition stage, in which the behaviors emerging in the danger zone become the norm when participants have a task or project to work on. Beliefs are embedded, and behaviors reflect the emergent norms of the group more than they do those of the parent organization. The second stage in Zone III is characterized by new ways of interfacing with the larger community by adoption of a permanent mode of behavior with the environment that is collaborative. The group now thinks collaboratively and true intergroup problem solving is the norm. Behaviors in Zone III alter the operations of the

parent organization by causing them to think collaboratively. Their
boundaries are no longer separate entities, but overlapping structures that deal with the world synergistically. These become true
learning organizations, which think as a community, problem solve
together, are future oriented, and integrate operations.

If a collaboration is desired, optimal movement is from Zone I
through Zone III. In this project, we spent a lot of time in the danger zone, and the leap toward Zone III was not tried by everyone.
Perhaps it takes one or two people to take the first step for others to
follow. This is where we seem to be with this project at the time of
writing this book. For some, there is no sense returning to what was
before. The separate structures were not effective in solving the problems faced by schools and communities, which are constantly changing. The belief that what we have been doing is effective and will be
effective in the future just perpetuates the habitus that denies the
opportunity for cultural growth of communities. Therefore, those
who have made the transition in their beliefs and understandings
must venture back and forth over the divide to convert and engage
others in the new. Then we all participate as a learning community
and can begin to approach the future, which is less based on the past
than it is on the unknown.

The Proposal: As Postscript, As Beginning

I expected this project to be completed long ago. I wanted to end
this book with the finished proposal, but, as of March 1995 the
proposal has not been presented to the School Board. The architect
has been chosen, and the Memorandum of Agreement, finally approved by lawyers representing the school system and the university,
has been scheduled for final going-over and signing sometime in
April. The lease agreement was a primary symbol of delay for the
past few months. The catch-22 was that the proposal was not finished (all the pieces were in place except formatting and additions
from the school system that only they could make) because it was
dependent on the lease agreement. But, as early as September we
were told that DCPS assigned a member of the Steering Committee
to work on nothing else in order to prepare and format the proposal.
In early October I met with her, and we agreed finally to take care of
the few missing pieces. I wrote the educational impact statement for

students, staff effectiveness, parent and community involvement, and the reporting of student progress to be appended to the proposal. She was to add the demographics, and a secretary from DCPS was to put the proposal in the correct format.

The plan was for copies of this finished product to be distributed by myself to our participants on the Steering Committee and DCPS would do likewise for their representatives. The same would be done for the union representative, then waivers necessary for inclusion in the proposal would be identified. The lawyers from both sides, however, were still looking at the wording of the Memorandum of Agreement, which must either accompany or precede the proposal to the School Board. The reality was that they had not finished their additions and the formatting had not been done. I believe that this phase of the project will soon conclude. We then face a minimum of eighteen months of construction, which follows bids and awarding of contracts.

Why such a long delay especially at the end of the process? First, there has been a crisis in the state concerning other priorities. There has been a large impact on the school system of immigrant children, who must be provided services at a time of major cutbacks in funding and support. Attempts to get the federal government to financially support increasing costs evaporated with the last election and the current proposals for further budget cuts and restructuring. In addition, other building projects have priorities that take precedence over this project. But, the most important source of delay has been a structural retreat from the progress we had made to work together at the decision-making level. Again habitus and convention, norms of behavior, and power wielding rose to meliorate the true goals and purpose of collaboration. Student, families, and communities became secondary when one side perceived the other had in some way insulted them or reneged on a promise. Our side had backed out of the opportunity to train a faculty member for Reading Recovery due to financial concerns. After going to the School Board with a proposal, we pulled out, and, quite frankly, they were not happy. There followed clear signs that they would and could delay this project, which is exactly what was happening. But, there are also signs that we are now moving forward. They have selected an architect, the Memorandum of Agreement is ready to be signed, and all expectation is that after this happens, the proposal will be formatted and with minor additions be finished. The process, although long, will proceed in earnest.

Indicators of Success

An analysis of the proposal from the perspective of the university clearly shows that we have achieved many of our goals. The proposal development involved many people from varied departments within the College of Education and from other colleges at the university. These persons, some for the first time, had the opportunity to work with and cooperatively develop and plan with individuals with whom they might never have worked if not for this project. Additionally, members of the university worked with DCPS, often with their own counterparts, and with community representatives. In many cases, relationships were forged that extended beyond this project. This provided newer faculty, in particular, a unique opportunity to make connections and develop relationships for their own service and research.

More importantly for the project itself, what we have created is a sustainable commitment to collaboration in the future. The spheres of influence have been changed, and there are new linkages of people working together in collaborative ways. The philosophy of the school is one of collegial governance and commitment to innovation and change. This goal is interconnected with the encouragement and support for on-site staff development and teacher training, research to improve classroom practice, and the development and dissemination of innovative methods and materials tested through research. Through the participation of FIU faculty from principal and staff interview and selection through the COMER model of facilitation of the school mechanisms, FIU will have the opportunity to forge new ground as an integral part of an ongoing collabortive effort long after the planning phase is over. As described in the proposal, "The adoption of the COMER Process is a commitment on the part of all the stakeholders that the spirit of collaboration which has evolved in the planning stages of this school will continue with the awareness that the process implies constant evolution as the school tries to become a model COMER school." It is the sustainability that is the true test of this collaboration, and the opportunity has been built into the proposal. All we have to do is deliver on the commitment we have made.

In addition to the elements described in Chapter 6 and the interactive research model, there are elements of the proposal that clearly meet our wants and needs. The curriculum part of the proposal is constructivist in orientation and to be developed through interdisciplinary units and delivered in multiage student groupings. The physical plant will support the three developmental communities described in the curriculum. High-technology linkages will allow communication between the school and the college staff. FIU staff will provide course work, in-service, and advanced degree program coursework on site or in close proximity to the school. We also will be fully involved in the community linkage component to promote family/community involvement as described in a previous chapter.

Analysis of the proposal from the perspective of the school district shows that they have accomplished what they always set out to accomplish: building an elementary school to relieve overcrowding in the existing schools that surround the FIU area. The population of the school when it opens will probably be largely immigrant and Hispanic. The nationalities of the student population are varied— originating from Central and South America with the dominant groups being Cuban-American and Nicaraguan-American immigrants. These are just two of the growing subcultures represented in Dade County. The school system faces needs that are more unique than there are models of resolution for in other parts of the United States. Therefore, innovative configurations and solution-seeking collaborations are supported and encouraged.

The basic structures of operation of a DCPS elementary school have been retained. The COMER model is being implemented in varying stages in at least thirteen other sites, so this is less of a divergence from operations than it seems. Of course what is unique here is that COMER is being implemented from preopening with the facilitation ongoing with the trained FIU faculty member. DCPS is interested in success through achievement, and this site brings together elements that have not been tried in combination before.

This project should never be over. The completion of the proposal is merely a step along the way and cannot solely be used to predict success or failure. Those elements can only be determined over time by criteria of continued involvement of representatives in the transorganizational alliance. What they accomplish and whether the linkages can be sustained in the future for further collaboration will be the real determinants of success. Indications are that the project has affected the spheres of influence between and within each organization. Only further analysis over time, however, will tell if the innovation can outlast the leadership of each organization, whether the metaphors of each organization changed, if the new interaction patterns have been integrated into the operation of the COE, and whether the public school system now images a future that includes the university.

There are some indications of success. Other negotiations are proceeding from the context of this project and the same people are being involved based on the evolving history of collaboration. We have created the new symbols, myths, and rituals of an emerging culture. We even have started to tell stories that are collective; the one about Yale, Comer training, nineteen inches of snow, and being stranded in a restaurant without a way back to the hotel is my favorite! Evolving are new models for long-range planning, models that are based on trust and respect. But, this is a cardboard house with little ascribed legitimacy, and a house of cards easily can be blown down. If trust and respect are not maintained, if authenticity in relationships is not promoted, or if positions of power and circles of influence once again become barriers to reform efforts, we could easily lose the shared vision of collaboration. We could all easily revert to the habitus, and the school culture with its mode of operation will continue to replicate itself as it has done in the past.

What I learned from this project differs from what the organization learned. First, it is not enough to have a personal vision; you must focus energies. You have to develop patience to see reality objectively. You have to encourage growth and the capacity to learn in individuals as well as in organizations. Collaboration is not sustained without the personal interchanges. People make the changes, initiate them and sustain them. Second, the analysis and perspective presented in this analysis are merely images of reality, not truth itself. These images enhance and illuminate a view of the world (like the t-shirt that says a "New York View of the World"; you can see the rest of the world from the horizon, but up close you view the world in relationship only to New York). This point of view is personal. It is my interpretation of our walk in the woods together. What is important is whether the next project and the next participants begin from the new history, continue the dialogue, continue the relationships, and continue the trust.

The idea of point of view, or making one's own landscape of understanding, is described by Greene (1978, 2) as follows:

I take from the philosopher Maurice Merleau-Ponty the idea that the life of reason develops against a background of perceived realities, that to remain in touch with one's original perceptions is to be present to oneself. A human being lives, as it were, in two orders—one created by his or her relations with the perceptual fields that are given in experience, the other created by his or her relations with a human social environment. It is important to hold in mind, therefore, that each of us achieved contact with the world from a particular vantage point, in terms of a particular biography. All of this underlies our present perspectives and affects the way we look at things and talk about things and structure our realities. To be in touch with our landscapes is to be conscious of our evolving experiences, to be aware of the ways in which we encounter the world.

If each of these organizations and the people who work in them have learned nothing else but to appreciate, respect, and understand that each person perceives individually and that this is not only acceptable but also desired, then we have made progress toward new forms of working together.

This is just the beginning. True collaboration does not end with a document and a ceremony. It evolves and changes as new players come in, some players leave, and the project itself faces new realities. Those of us on the Steering Committee live and work in a changing environment, in step and out of step with the rest of the state and the rest of the country. We have been told we are forging new ground in Miami, the city of the future that is not terribly old. We have the opportunity to make anything we desire because we do not follow a set blueprint. No place is quite like our place. The best hope for a successful future, for schools, universities, communities, and families, is through cooperation and collaboration. Let's begin together.

Chapter Eight
Community Solutions

Characteristics of a Community

In an ideal world, communities would exist and operate as integrated wholes, serving with dignity and in the best interests of the population they represent. They would be in alignment with the real world, creating conditions for accomplishing the goals identified by the constructs that helped define that community. This condition of alignment refers to the micro and macrostrategies used to deal with the real world. At the basic level is the environment with the external constraints imposed by the unique conditions of place and time. We operate on and in that environment through our behavior—through actions that are congruent or incongruent with the environment. If behavior is out of alignment with the environment, one or the other must adapt or change. Of course, community environments are less likely to change than are individual behaviors. It is the congregate of similar individual behaviors that synergistically creates conditions for community changes. When behaviors do not align with environmental expectations, people withdraw if there is no support or they may seek legislated solutions. This doesn't create long-lasting environmental changes. Individual behavior is guided by cognitive maps and strategies, by the construction of the world as it is perceived. These are the capabilities available in the repertoire of individuals and groups to accomplish their goals. These capabilities are organized by our belief systems, which drive the choices of which capabilities to use to resolve conflicts so that resolution is in alignment with time and place. Together these elements reflect community identity, the metaphor of the collective environment, behavior, capabilities, and values evident within people and the communities of which they are a part (Dilts, 1990).

The relationship between beliefs, capabilities, and behavior is the alignment between self-efficacy and expectations. Bandura's construct of self-efficacy suggests that bringing to consciousness the unconscious beliefs about ability and competence changes an individual's sense of what he or she is capable of. It changes the personal identity he or she has concerning competence and life-direction. Thus, beliefs are generalizations about relationships between experiences including causal relations, meaning relationships, and capabilities. They are representations in our cognitive scheme that direct future behavior. The same is true of communities. Effective communities are those whose sense of capability is congruent with the actions they take to support the populations that are part of their environment. Communities too must reflect efficacy and be aware of the alignment between beliefs, goals, and expectations and the reality of operating in an environment that may be changing.

The psychological sense of community is a transient experience, which is preceded or followed by some kind of conflict or tension. The people who make up the community respond to this tension either by maintaining their behaviors and perpetuating the environment or by altering their environment through alternative behaviors. Decisive consideration for action is the maintenance of a sense of community (Saranson, 1974, 273). But, that community can evolve into new forms if the actions are directed toward a state that is more relevant to the needs of the people. Participants may also choose to give up their selfhood to the priority needs of society in order for it to survive. Group values then would supersede self-values and the result, like that of the community in utopian schemes, moves that collective vision forward. Whether or not that happens, community involves people, and the quality of the relationships between them sustains the social interactions and structural connections that provide, in Durkheim's terms, the *social glue* that holds society together and creates, maintains, and sustains a forward-looking collective conscience (Schwab, 1982, 348, 380).

For the individual and the collective to be adaptive requires an approach that is a process, or a retraining, that occurs as a result of reflection on the problem solving and critical thinking individuals use and whether, when brought to the cognitive awareness level, alignment of these skills can alter how tasks are approached. Alignment is the cognitive construct representing integration of all the background and environmental factors that lead to the successful strategies; it is the state of being of the fully integrated dimensions of environment, behavior, capabilities, beliefs, and personal identity used in formal and informal dealings with the real world. Full alignment means that behavior is consistent with these dimensions. Difficulties exist when the repertoire of behavior does not include ways to deal with the environment, or strategies and maps that generate behavior consistent with their goals are not formulated. This creates, in Festinger's terms, *cognitive dissonance:* a conflict of belief with outcome. Using Bandura's model of efficacy and the Piagetian theory of accommodation and assimilation, the activation of capabilities and beliefs in congruence with goal direction must be a precursor for alignment and success of individuals and communities.

What are the conditions of alignment for the individual as a member of the community? What would be needed to motivate community members toward alignment, and what stops this movement from occurring? First, we need to look at the function of communities and what has been done to create, support, and in some cases, purposefully and incidentally dissolve them.

The Function and Form of a Community

A classic in community discussion is the Goodman and Goodman (1960, 19) work called *Communitas.* The authors described the function of a community as integrated with its form; thus, the critique of that form, whether physical or emotional, is that it must function for the good. Is it worthwhile, worthy, and compatible with the people and the esthetics of the community it serves? Rather than fit the individual to the plan, the plan should evolve from the wants, needs, and collective desires of the people who will live in and participate in the community's further growth and evolution. The community elements Goodman and Goodman consider for decision making related to structure include technology, the relation of work and leisure, domestic life, education of children and adults, esthetics, political initiatives, and economic institutions. Thus the plan must be cognizant of the interrelatedness of these elements, which combine to form the culture of the community.

This community plan is the utopian ideal. The reality is what Bourdieu (1993, 14) defined as habitus, or a feel for the game; the structured and unstructured dispositions that generate practice. Community essence is too often the result of cultural production that is structured by the possession of economic and/or political capital, often envisaged in symbolic form. The forces impacting on this are external and internal. The domination of culture by the status of the dominant class (37) is aided by an education system that reproduces legitimate consumption. It is not just the institutionalism of public education; colleges and universities and learned societies also contribute to legitimization external to the beliefs and dispositions of the local community itself. They impose sanctions through the engendering of a cooperative stance by consecration of behaviors and a certain type of work ethic for those who seek to be legitimized by their endorsement. They legitimize the criteria of inclusion that may or may not be appropriate to the community, yet, by some divine authority the players themselves bend to the criteria of certification, making each community more like the others than representative of the distinct characteristics that make it functionally unique. Solutions to community problems are sought through the collective vision that is imposed from without. This creates a sameness seen from community to community and school to school. Solutions are common solutions. They have been tried elsewhere where they have achieved success and have been imported intact to a new place. The reality of communities is that environments are no longer predictable and solutions that are school based are no longer a natural part of the community in which the school resides. Systematic coordinated efforts to create a culture of community support and a climate of relationships that work toward common goals require time, skills, and energies that we no longer seem to have the luxury to sustain.

Numerous examples of attempts to create community solutions have their origins in state and federal initiatives. For example, in Florida there has been a legislated attempt to coordinate and create a shared vision of reform requiring community participation. Blueprint 2000 is state legislation the intent of which is to raise standards and return the responsibility for education to those closest to the students: the school, teachers, and parents. There is no university involvement as described in the document. How can there be a community revolving around schools without a definition of a university role as a partner in implementation? The reform, however, calls for parents, students, teachers, administration, and business and community members—those local decision makers on school advisory councils—to bring about systemic reform. For Miami, solutions are often out of step with the larger community needs and the problem is often fueled by the self-interest of those who have amassed a larger part of the political and economic power.

Where do we go from here if large-scale solutions are dominated by partisanship and the community solutions have often become legislative? "Sincerity . . . is only possible—and only achieved— when there is a perfect and immediate harmony between the expectations inscribed in the position occupied . . . and the dispositions of the occupant" (Bourdieu, 1993, 95). What Bourdieu described as harmony is presented here as alignment. If the historical, persistent behaviors continue after the moment of need is over, they become the myths of organizational behavior and the norms of community perspective; they reproduce individual behaviors that are no longer tied to the enactment of beliefs and capabilities. They become outmoded and obsolete and perpetuate the status quo as obstacles for true collaboration.

Bourdieu (1993, 123) spoke about the reproduction of culture, the consecration of cultural consumption, and the elevation of legitimate knowledge through educational curricular choices. This was evident in the attempts during this project of each of the parent organization participants to continue to operate as they had in the past without awareness that what they were doing was perpetuating the habitus and disallowing cultural evolution to occur. This was reflected in the maintenance of structural integrity of the school architecture, of the administrative rules and regulations that could not and would not be altered, and of the union restrictions on personnel and training. Changes are slow, and this contributes to the maintenance of the status quo, of culture, knowledge, practice, and routine, all rationalized by maintenance and inculcation of process, both rational and empirical. The leap across the Zone II danger zone depicted in Chapter 7 requires a commitment to change, which includes the very cultural artifacts of the organization—the language, myths, rituals, roles, and behaviors that are structural products of the historical realities of the economic and social conditions of production. Schooling perpetuates the historic reality, but if it is not clear or is fictional, the result is the perpetuation of a canon of belief, of literature, or of knowledge that loses relevancy to time and place. To understand is to recognize the worldview of the social group that produces the history. This includes the political, ethical, and structural positions and the ability to transform, subvert, or preserve that habitus. You can't win if you don't enter the game. You can't move to Zone III and become part of a learning organization if there is not the altering of strategies that successfully leads to community solutions. This is only accomplished by understanding the relationship of the environment, behaviors, capabilities, and beliefs that together evolve as the community identity.

Not surprisingly, past attempts toward relevance for communities have created further dissolution of them. These efforts have systematically legislated the dissolution of communities. There is now no vehicle to solve community problems, only legislated opportunities for individual solutions. An example of this is busing, which has taken away the web of interrelatedness that allowed a forum for community dissemination of information and cohesion through common participation in the education of children. The legislated solution to segregation has removed the school as the focal point of community relevance in favor of systemwide mandates and compliance-driven structures. In Miami, the third largest system of public education in the United States, this structure, as described previously, maintains high compliance. We have legislated away equity in the name of equal opportunity of access. The dissolving of community ties was done with one fell swoop of the legislative pen as students, teachers, parents, and neighborhoods lost control of their schools to large bureaucratic structures far removed from the realities of neighborhood need. The family of concern became an adoptive family without portraits of what the members looked like. This loss of faces was replaced by numbers, and solutions for problems became solutions for the masses. We no longer talk about the individual child, but of the group of which they are a part: exceptional education, Chapter I, at-risk, gifted, average, talented, on and on. Where are their portraits now?

Reform Mandates

Reform movements that have been tried in the past at localized sites have recognized problems in replication when they have tried to "scale-up" (Olson, 1994). In systematically disseminating and replicating projects and reform initiatives in diverse communities across the country, issues of maintaining the integrity of the effort and essence of the reform have surfaced as legitimate concerns. Successful replication requires firstly that proof be given that the program is doing what it purports to be doing and that the desired effect is being achieved. Then, careful planning can occur to export the project and engender community support, resources, funding, site-based leadership, and technical assistance (Olson, 1994, 43). Prescriptive solutions may be doomed to failure if changes in teacher knowledge and beliefs are not incorporated into the effort. The measures of success must include teacher ability to collaborate to improve the climate for instruction in partnership with the innovation, district, and university support network, all through a process that is fully participative.

According to Comer (1980, xiv), "Our political, social and economic institutions tended to expect the public schools to take on these missions without adequate back-up of resources or the priorities necessary for such innovations. Educators, viewing their primary tasks as enabling children to acquire the methods and content of learning and socializing, frequently have been concerned that these additional social, political and psychological objectives of schooling will impair the school's capacity to achieve its primary mission." Therefore, "genuine collaboration and systematic change were necessary for the public school in the 60s, and are so today. Conflicting interest, lack of knowledge and skill, and inadequate schooling structures resulted in the late 60s and 70s in a growing skepticism about collaborations that were not authentic. Parents also learned painfully and bitterly the 'change' or 'new' is not necessarily better."

Comer (1980, xvi) defined collaboration as, "That special relationship in which all engage directly in a common enterprise, assuming roles not only appropriate to training, and skill, but fashioned cooperatively to serve the general welfare." This requires the sharing of expertise because there are structural considerations, relationship reasons, conflict caused by perceived differences in status among collaborators, use of the other organization and the history of that use, all making it difficult to alter perceptions, style, and method of problem solving. Adding to this conflict are the reward system of the college and university; teacher pressure from external sources, such as parents, politicians, and media, for positive accountability; stereotypes; perceptions of behavior requiring altering expectations in order to establish trust; sharing of expertise; roles of school staff and administration, supervisors, and so forth; and successful, competent teachers (213).

Teacher Professionalization

The area that purports to take the greatest effort in collaboration between universities and school districts is that of teacher preparation and the continuing professional development of teachers. Teacher training and post-training inculcation are areas in which a dichotomy exists between individual needs, district needs, college specifications, and community expectations. Stallings (1991, 1992), Lieberman (1990), and Sirotnik and Goodlad (1988) have written extensively about collaborative initiatives that would link teacher preparation programs to community needs in order to enhance relevance and produce effective results. Their examples are in the establishment of linkages between colleges or universities and school districts to collectively prepare professionals for changing work environments. The recent literature on professional development schools is focused on preparing future teachers to share in the decision making and responsibilities for carrying out programmatic goals. Stallings (1991) advocated a relationship between student teachers, supervising teachers, and college supervisors to together produce teachers responsive to the unique environmental needs of inner-city schools. Results of her research show that a supportive responsive environment produces changes in classroom teachers. In another report of results, Stallings (1992) suggested that representatives of each institution serve on joint councils that provide weekly seminars for participants, jointly planned and delivered by college supervisors and teachers in school. When the environment is safe and the staff is committed to self-growth and the goals of the project, then the college faculty can collaborate with the school staff, making sure that the program is successful. This also results in a supportive community that can address changing needs while engaging participants in a cooperative, collaborative mode of solution finding. As seen in the narrative of this case study, that is a tremendously complicated thing to accomplish. It requires a commitment that is supra-institutional. It necessitates university administration willing to assign and/or support faculty to participate at the school site in order for involvement to be sustained. As seen previously, this commitment to provide faculty time to participate in any model of community collaboration is critical to maintaining and sustaining the truth and perception that all stakeholders are represented in the ongoing day-to-day reality of the project.

Strategies to create communities of those involved in projects that explore better preparation of teachers and postservice renewal must engender the support and involvement of the university in the process. Collegial consultation focused on problems of practice not only can create collaborative solutions aimed toward community building, but also firmly establish that the process has created an environment where the voices of all constituents are recognized as legitimate parts of that community. Rhetoric about this type of collaboration is the result of ever-increasing demands on schools. The reality of schooling today is the need to accomplish multiple goals—to produce higher levels of student performance, to celebrate diversity, to show evidence of student learning that includes the ability to create, critically analyze, apply, produce, and invent solutions (Darling-Hammond, ed., 1994, 5). This requires teachers skilled beyond the level that is currently in place in teacher education programs. Those already in the field require renewal. Darling-Hammond contended that discipline expertise is not enough, particularly in nontraditional classrooms. Of course, the question of whether a traditional classroom exists anymore is one that certainly is an issue, particularly in Miami. The solution is professional development schools that feature collaboration, shared participation in the decision-making teams and processes within the school, and continued collaborative research for improvement that is site specific (9).

This requires the restructuring of university programs with an emphasis on professional development from undergraduate through graduate programs, much in alignment with the national accrediting society's agenda. This is needed not only for teachers preservice but also for in-service teachers for whom traditional models of retraining and continued support have not been systemic. The goal is the establishment of a sense of efficacy in the process and the recognition that old solutions are no longer viable in changing communities. Collaboration, then, is seen as continuous learning for all.

This perspective of continued development for teachers has evolved from dialogue about the abilities and skills of those who enter into teaching. Lanier and Little (1986, 563) described teaching as a short-term, low-commitment occupation that requires few intensive, coherent educational provisions. The practice of teaching requires behaviors that may not be part of training programs, including the roles required to interact with administration, parents, and community. Further, the context and uniqueness of individual classrooms is often overlooked in initial teacher preparation while other aspects related to licensing and beginning teacher programs are overorchestrated. Teachers operate in isolated workplaces; they find themselves compartmentalized. Teachers are not autonomous and have no opportunity or obligation to contribute to solutions for organizational problems. Schools are not organized to promote inquiry and for teachers to reflect on practice. Instead, they engage in trial-and-error learning (561). Lanier and Little (1986, 560) suggested that the school community support continued teacher education through the professional development of practicing teachers to meliorate the contradiction between professional ideals and the reality of the workplace so as to reinforce lifelong learning. Primary in this quest is to create a supportive collaborative climate. This orientation is exactly that which prompted the participants in this project to stick with it to try to create an environment where practice is combined with theory and training. This school, when completed, could provide the integration of training and practice needed for relevance in the field of teacher professional training. The involvement described in the proposal mission was not a compromise. It was a fundamental recognition that preservice and postservice support was necessary to meet the evolving needs of this community.

This climate of support must be cognizant of the regularities embedded in schools that either have to be circumvented or changed. These include how people relate to one another, the use of solutions that are prescriptive rather than mutually adaptable, and the ability to act locally and utilize professional capabilities and dispositions within the related organizations to create solutions that are specific to the site (James, 1991, 170–172). As James noted (172), we sometimes have to protect ourselves from governmental rules, regulations, and procedures when they no longer serve the purpose they were intended to protect. That is the message of communitarianism. We need to create solutions ourselves for problems that cannot be legislatively solved.

Conley (1991) described areas to which community members should turn their attention. First is the structure of the organization and who participates in decision making, the types of decisions in which members may participate, and the degree of centralization in the organization where decisions are approved (226). Second, what are the aims of participation? Does participation serve the bureaucratic structure of one of the members? Is it for buy-in of participants? Is it political representation, or is it culture creating? (228) Third, are participants changing roles from their parent organization or from traditional expectations? If so, the domain of their involvement may be new territory for them. Do they want to participate, what is at stake if they do, and what are the requirements and skills necessary for them to interact effectively? (231) Fourth, what support is available to structure relationships between individuals in the newly formed group? What are the resources available? How will success be determined, and what formative measures will monitor ongoing performance of individuals and the group as a whole? Can decision-making lines of authority be redefined? Will traditional forms of participation be established? (240–244)

School problems have become demographic, racial, statistical complexities rather than community problems. Judgment of success is by the norm, the bell curve, the canon of acceptable, appropriate, politically correct messages all at the loss of talking about the individual. It is not just the loss of the child. It is also the loss of parental knowledge and involvement. This is one of the rationales for the COMER project. These types of solutions actively engender the involvement and collaboration of the community with firsthand interest in the life of the school. This life is not just for the students; it is also for the parents, teachers, neighborhoods, and well-being of all who seek to better this institution and remember the humaneness of having it as a focal point of congregation. Models of community, such as COMER, rely on the building-up of communities and on the consensual nature of efforts to make change through collaboration in decision-making processes. The three elements—the beliefs that guide the process—are collaboration, consensus, and a no-fault philosophy. The latter is the most interesting, since it removes the finger pointing from the process and allows movement toward accomplishing goals without dwelling on and endorsing the systemic problems of the past that inhibited the process. If the process continues in good faith, the alignment of environment, behavior, capabilities, and beliefs can occur so that schools become communities that have relevant identities. What follows is a description of the environment of Miami. It is presented so that the reader can assess whether the school community effort can be redefined so that community solutions become viable.

An Example: The Miami Community

Portes and Stepick (1993) contended that Miami is like no other place. It is not, they asserted, a microcosm of the U.S. city, nor is it a global financial city (Sassen, 1991) either. It never was, and yet its brief history has led it to the point today where it is an experiment and possibly a portent of cities of the future. Miami is an open door to change; the business class is composed increasingly of immigrants who came here over the past thirty years; small business is localized and immigrant controlled, segregated to serve a particular subculture; a mainstream is not apparent as parallel growth structures create their own system of class, mobility, and institutional life; acculturation has occurred in reverse as the parallel social systems have emerged in a bicultural environment (Portes and Stepick, 1993, 8–9). These factors have created competing discourses of how and where Miami is going. Each subculture (the pre-Mariel Cubans, post-Mariel Cubans, Nicaraguans, Haitians, Blacks, and whites) has squared off in the competition for limited resources and political and economic pieces of the pie. There have clearly been winners and losers here.

The loss of hegemony by those who were here the longest has contributed to the dissolution of the community and the loss of the individual to the blur of group caricature. "The transformation of the political order is taking place in a context where the rupture of the old hegemonic discourse has not yet given rise to a new one . . . The result is that several mutually unintelligible perceptual "maps" coexist in the same physical space . . . the existence of these . . . plays back on everyday reality, leading to more stereotypical behavior by members of the different communities . . . (who) lead their lives in separate worlds, but when meeting each other in public places they tend to adopt a ritualized stance, influenced by their own particular discourse" (Portes and Stepick, 1993, 212).

Miami power brokers are involved in the quest to see Miami become a global city—not the social construction of a global city, but Sassen's view of the global city as the center of financial and international activity, such as New York, Tokyo, or London. Can Miami become this? Required is an infrastructure of service transactions, specialized advertising, accounting, and management consulting to support this. None of this is congruent with the present-day Miami economic and political climate. Those three cities have evolved as financial players in spite of the population and at the expense of the population. The result has been the flight of the middle class, which has left the city to the poor, the homeless, the unemployed, and, at the other extreme, the upper-class group working for the financial community. Thus, the financial success is independent of the community in which it geographically resides. Growth also requires the use of advanced technology and involves a highly educated populace, a raising of the quality of life, and accompanying jobs for the rest of the population. In Miami, the enlightened elite is separated by a subculture structure resulting from the immigration patterns and rapid growth in population. We are not one community, and yet we are governed and educated by rationales that are monolithic. Thus, when we try to create solutions that are encompassing, we, in effect, dissolve the ties that bind communities together. If Bourdieu is correct, the relationship and opportunity exist in education to transcend the loss of community by creating educational solutions that reverse the trend. These solutions involve all those who have a stake in building communities that meet our criteria of alignment. The vehicle for this can be a reformulated system of education of students built on a structure of teacher training that breaks the ties to past practices that are not constructive or supportive of communities.

Redefining the School Community

The coming together of the players in the project described in this narrative was the result of an opportunity to create a break-the-mold school as part of a proposal to obtain funding through New America Schools Development Corporation, a response to the America 2000 national initiative. Since I conceived of the integration of community support used to provide the focus for the project, I would like to relate the story I told to the representatives of each organization at the first meeting.

As an exceptional education specialist for an emotionally handicapped cluster in a public school system, daily I was faced with the reality that school problems do not exist in isolation from home, family, and community problems. A story I tell is of the day when a student, the youngest of five children, came to school and by the time he reached his classroom had already started two fights, one on the bus coming to school, the other in the cafeteria. He sauntered into his classroom, put his head down on the desk, and began to cry. He left his home that morning while his mother, the only adult in the home, was being evicted. He did not know whether to take the bus home or where she would be when he got there. As a good public servant I was obligated to legitimize his disclosure. I did.

The family counselor and I drove over to his home. All the belongings of the family were on the street (sparse though they were); his mother, a petite woman, was standing outside the door to the apartment arguing with the slumlord. The family counselor and I offered to help her. We drove over to the social service agency, which was nearby (such agencies are housed physically within the neighborhoods of need), to talk to her caseworker. He told us that he knew she was being evicted and that she did not "do" what was necessary to apply and obtain support to pay her rent. Why, we asked, were we not informed? Wasn't this a matter that went beyond his agency and involved everyone who worked with and for these family members? Shouldn't this family be afforded the collective resources and integration of services that each agency could bring to bear if they worked together and desisted in duplication of information? That morning five children were sent off to various schools without notifying any school personnel that they would have no place to return to at the end of the day. He said that it was not part of his responsibility, but, now that we had informed him, he would have a representative pick the children up and put them in shelters; in effect, he was removing them from the home because they now had no roof over their heads. Frustrating as this may seem, when I got back to my school site, my responsibility was to inform the schools attended by the other children. The school day ended. All the children were picked up and taken to shelters, but they were not placed together. The boys went to one shelter, the girls to another; and days later, through my own resources within the school system, I found out where they were eventually enrolled.

By then the mother moved in with her aunt in the northern part of the neighboring county. I called her and she was frantic. She did not know and was never informed where the five children were taken and had no contact with them. The oldest eventually called her from a pay phone at his new school, but she was not informed by the authorities as to their whereabouts or well-being. The family counselor and I volunteered to pick her up and take her to visit the children at their schools. We did. We also took her to take a drug test, fill out the forms, and process the papers necessary to get her children back. The obstacles, to her, seemed insurmountable. She had no job, no money, and the support she had been receiving from AFDC (Aid for Families with Dependent Children) stopped when she lost her home and the children were taken into custody.

I can't tell you what happened to this family. I can tell you that the system failed. The lack of communication between the agencies responsible for support of families is apparent, but the secrecy and protectiveness with which they harbor information pertinent to all and withhold it from each other is incomprehensible. Two days after we helped this mother visit her children, they all ran away. I assume they were reunited. I hope they could start all over. When rules and regulations serve the persistence of bureaucratic structures rather than the people they were meant to help, some people understandably circumvent them.

The Community Vision

How can these problems be addressed? That was the intention of the original proposal. The goals of the original proposal led to the conceptualization of a new learning environment supportive of the changing needs of children and families and of the structures necessary to support them. The theme of the project was interdependence through shared involvement and included a community-support mechanism and a parent education program supportive of children and families. We envisioned a preschool component to ensure that all children enter school ready to learn, integrated curriculum relevant to the needs and interests of students and the community, teacher training that included extensive experience prior to employment to ensure no teacher was a beginning teacher, and opportunity for experienced teachers to engage in continuous learning. This required a governance structure that was collaborative and engaging of all stakeholders.

The purposes of the project were to enable and encourage people to take control of their own stake in quality education and to create collaborative educational settings, especially in urban public school environments. These interests were represented by students, parents, teachers, administrators, and the community of colleges and universities that educate teachers; business and industry, which desire an educated workforce and knowledgeable consumers; and public and private agencies that provide support to the educative process.

What is the makeup of this proposed school community? Part of this proposal was a redefinition of that community to include health and social services and community and family support at the school site. Coordination would occur through a natural environment of the school site. This made the school site the physical focus to unite the community. Preschool early intervention, model child care, and case planning involving business, schools, and service agencies were part of that community. A curriculum that transcended the fragmentation of knowledge by subject area was proposed, conceived as interdisciplinary in nature, and to be serviced through multiage flexible groupings in an activity-based instructional mode. Teacher training for this required specialized knowledge that was community oriented and recognized family and health support necessary for students to learn.

Why was a reconceptualization necessary? The problems of this area and those of the majority of urban areas require new solutions. What has worked for communities in the past are not viable solutions for today. The elements under consideration were problems of a diverse racial, ethnic, cultural, and social mix creating a challenging setting. Social changes had to be redefined from racial and ethnic conflict, which is political, and those of poverty resulting from displacement, crime, substance abuse, and disenfranchisement. Predictions for the future of this area are for more minorities, more Hispanics, more diversity of culture and language, and social isolation.

My contribution to the proposal is paraphrased as follows:

Achieving the goals of the national and local initiatives for reform can occur only when the linkages among the interdependent participants and beneficiaries are securely in place and operationally productive. This requires community support, parental awareness, educational involvement, and a structure of support services that includes the community, businesses, and governmental and private social service and health agencies. This becomes the school community.

Isolation of programs prevents the integration of services into a synergistic whole. The problems of families at risk do not exist in isolation from one another, nor are they confined to the family unit, whatever the makeup of that unit. They become community problems and they require community solutions. To reduce the risk for children and families, reduction in parent isolation and help in acquiring knowledge about and negotiating in the outside world and among service agencies are necessary. Increasingly larger numbers of people require and qualify for these services. We must redefine and redesign schools to incorporate and facilitate access to these services for students and their families.

The establishment of links from old structures to the new models of service requires planning and collaboration. The planning required includes the creation of models and methods that result in partnership among the stakeholders; modifications to the design of training for staff that supports new models, stimulation of volunteerism and engendering interest in those who have not participated in the process before; promotion of private sector involvement and active participation; design of delivery systems that are congruent with the newly formulated goals; and the development of new models for community support.

This requires new organizational structures based upon the individual character of the school/family/community. This reformulated structure can begin to meet the evolving needs of a multicultural, multilingual, urban environment, provide for integrated support for the family, and meet the needs of the community. This requires a refocusing of roles and responsibilities for school administration, redefining the role of principal from manager and curricular leader to director or coordinator of the linkages required for interdependence of operation; staffing by a professional population committed to new goals and responsibilities; community and parent involvement in the day-to-day operation of a school; a parent information and dissemination clearinghouse in operation at the site; parent engagement with the school and understanding of how the school operates (the demystification of the school); volunteerism and intergenerational support.

The service component should bring to the school site services that now require applications elsewhere. Referral for services could come from any area, e.g., education, counseling services, or community school. Primary is health care services that are integrated into the site through an agency liaison on staff. This requires new roles and a redefinition of existing roles, the development of models of service support within each school that link directly with the community setting, planning for sharing of resources rather than diffusion of support, and implementation of technological support and informational access between and across agencies directly to families and communities.

Counseling support services for parents and adults should include workshops on student learning for parents to acquire techniques of support to enhance their children's school success; parents learning in parallel with their preschoolers; family dynamics counseling for family members; consumer education; literacy and job-skill training, career counseling and life skill training; clearinghouse for information and networking with family agencies in the larger community. Students could receive on-site referral and testing, and counseling support services along with drug and alcohol prevention education. This component requires the development and designing of team-building models and activities to support delivery of cooperative collaborative behaviors. New service delivery models and contextual training for participatory parenting, and new linkages for utilization of expertise and for information dissemina-tion are needed.

The school as community integrates the other services into a full-time year-round facility that meets community needs. The elements of this cooperative include a preschool center and day-care program linked to education, social services, and counseling areas; after-school care fa-cility in an extended-school setting with summer recreational and edu-cational programs; public library outreach; adult education classes and community school literacy classes, G.E.D., language programs, voter reg-istration, and so on; programs directed toward new immigrants; senior center supporting intergenerational planning and involvement in edu-cation coordinated through this center; student services for tutoring, remediation, and classes in the arts. Models for integrating these services are needed, along with sources of financial support. Links to business and the public/private sector need to be established.

How should this new model be administered within the context of an operating public school system? A new model of administration would be needed with the principal acting as director of the integration of resources necessary for school success for students. Support staff includes persons responsible for counseling, preschool, mentors and community volunteers, and university support personnel committed to active in-volvement in the day-to-day operations of the school, student teachers, and the student training site.

A full-service school model that is organized as a cooperative ongo-ing effort of community/family/school for advocacy requires a new orga-nizational structure. This model is a jointly held trust among the facili-tating areas that impact on the education, health, and welfare of families and communities and the children who live in them.

Many of the elements that have been identified independently as necessary to produce measurable growth and educational gains are al-ready in place. What is different here is the planning for the linkages necessary for success. That involves redefinition of roles and responsibili-ties by staff, administration, and public and private sector organiza-tions. It requires a cooperative focus on the school/community as a com-munity supportive of families and the educational needs of children, as well as a community committed to being dynamic in meeting the chal-lenges in an evolving world. South Florida may predict the future for other parts of the country by its changing demography. We are already

experiencing what other schools will face. The solutions lie in redefining,
reforming, from birth to adulthood, the school/community of the future.

School System and University:
The Need for Communities

The plan above represents the ideal alignment of all participants, organizations, and community services necessary to collectively implement a successful environment supportive of learning and teaching. It was the starting point for the project described in the narrative preceding this chapter. Why wasn't this incorporated in total into the final proposal for the school on campus? First, this is an expensive program, one that relies heavily on funding. It is also expensive in the redefinition of individual and organizational beliefs concerning the way things should operate. As discussed previously, overcoming the organizational bureaucracy in favor of new structures and means of operation is very difficult, even when the rewards for such transformations outweigh the rationales for maintaining the status quo. Yet, our final proposal for the school had to be part of a process of changes in belief so that behaviors could align with those beliefs making environmental changes, however slowly they evolved. We have to move into Zone III, the integration of operations and the overlapping of the organizations that we represent, in order to think like a community and solve the emerging community needs.

Communities of support evolve structurally, but they also may be planned for, using strategies to implement the process of changes in beliefs in the people who work in them. The two primary structures that could unite and focus on the conditions necessary to implement environments supportive of the newly emerging environments for teaching and learning are the school system and the university. Using these two organizations as the focal point of change, the other agencies whose services are needed to fully serve educative environments can be mobilized and brought into a larger newly conceived community. As described in Chapter 2, these newer communities function as transorganizational environments, and the restrictions imposed by the functional history of each parent organization becomes less distinct.

Identification of the internal and external stakeholders is the first step in building these communities (Mason and Mitroff, 1989, 217–218). Stakeholders have their own resources, goals, and behavior patterns that distinguish their operational life. Sometimes this creates the primary barrier to community development as each guards against the elimination of the routine that characterizes their work life and legitimizes their operation. As people and organizations begin to work together, a network of interdependent relationships begins to develop between stakeholders. These relationships may be congruent with the goals of communal participation, but, often they are resistant. New strategies need to be developed between participants to permeate the organizational norm so that the resistant behaviors can be overcome. In reality, these resistant behaviors may be those that were rewarded by the organization in its traditional mode of operation. Thus, there must be changes in belief such that altering behavior gives more power to the organization through purposeful achievement of goals. The redefinition of goals gives the organization a reason to alter its traditional behavior patterns.

How can this be accomplished? There are numerous suggestions and methods to change behavior. At the most basic level is the commanding by superiors to act in certain ways. This task assignment strategy brings people together to work on a task, but, the task is usually specific to one set of problems or one goal. It does not change the relationship of one organization to another, nor does it, except informally, change the networking of the participants who view this as one more assignment, one more "thing" they must do. Bargaining, negotiating, and problem solving are other conversion strategies, but they too are transitory, task specific situations and, therefore, do not result in long-lasting change. The behaviors that typify these environments are those that coopt, absorb, avoid, or ignore some perspectives in favor of others. They are, as described earlier, power-coercive strategies whereby one point of view is adopted over the other because more authority is vested in that position by the organization standing behind it. Concession in the form of appeasement of some of the stakeholder's demands and the surrendering of others does not produce communities. It perpetuates the status quo while creating transitory changes, which do not address the underlying assumptions about the problem.

What we need in order to establish communities of support is the forming of an emotional bond and a commitment to change the way we operate and interface with each other. This requires walking in the shoes of the other stakeholders and actively seeking to understand their roles while forming new patterns of operation through the elimination of the organizational barriers that restrict such an interaction. Assumptions about past behavior and abilities of those working in separate structures are necessary in order to understand future actions and capabilities within new structural arrangements.

The creation of new strategies is the responsibility and cause of leadership. The mission must be clearly established so that all those who work toward teaching and learning environments that focus on students know what their identity is. This is a can-do mentality, one in which the barriers of organizations are overcome with the conviction that each agency is operating toward a similar goal and that the joining of resources, talent, and information is the most efficient and successful way to achieve those goals. It then becomes the responsibility of the managers of each agency to allocate resources and put the plans into practice in order to accomplish those goals.

This type of change is political and economic. When we talk about the primary community of school systems and universities, the political and economic reality is that each allocates resources and garners support from different sources. Each has established elaborate structures to handle the managing of the everyday life of their work. The established lines of information flow and the networking to obtain and communicate within and to other agencies is based on tradition. Schools aid the dissolution of community by an inherent institutionalism, which is directed toward testing and accountability, a pseudoprofessionalism measured in time spent in training, and teacher training that is based on recertification and licensing. Schools exist for purposes and functions that are exclusive of those of the university. Colleges and universities, likewise, serve a different purpose and function in ways that are unique to their structure. Therefore, the beliefs that each organization has about what is successful procedurally needs to be reconceived in light of new structures based on community solutions. What worked for one set of understandings and dispositions may not be operationally possible in the new model. Cooperation and collaboration require new ethical and moral outlooks that create conditions of freedom to operate and collaborate.

This may seem intractable or nonsolvable. It requires a socio-interaction and constructivist orientation within the culture of the organizations of stakeholders. It must be generated in the field by the participants as events are constructed, interpreted, and responded to. This imaging of the future is a creation that is generated together. The larger community learns together as they share suggestions for problems as they evolve. There is no blueprint for adaptation since, as I have argued previously, old solutions do not work. We now live and work in complexities where past behaviors do not align with new environmental problems and expectations for students and their families.

Two Roads to Travel

There are basically two ways to approach this problem. One is to assume that the dissolution of communities was inevitable and that it is in line with the evolution of modern society. There is much evidence to support this (Sassen, 1991), especially if we want to be globally competitive. Logically, then, solutions that aim at reclaiming what was lost are not worthwhile efforts since there is no proof that it is the future desired state. Problems attributed to the dissolution of communities, such as deterioration of neighborhoods and the loss of school as a focal point of community-supportive climates for education, are not causal, and attention and resources should be directed elsewhere. On the other hand, if this is not true and if communities of old held together supportive networks that promoted beliefs and values that were integral to the formation of a collective culture that we desire to reclaim, then we must direct our efforts toward community building as a viable solution. The reality is that we cannot do anything less. The first option promotes inaction, and we are painfully aware who the losers will be. The second option provides opportunities. As options are explored in the second scenario, some will be more viable than others, but in the act of exploration creative solutions and innovations will take shape.

Chapter Nine
Creating Conditions for Growth

In the preceding chapters I have tried to describe the research, theory, and practice of creating the conditions that support and sustain a collaborative endeavor between school systems and universities. The case study provided the structure for analysis of the issues and problems that pervade this type of participation. The overriding purpose for me, however, was to provide a forum for discussion of some of the issues at work in both environments that limit opportunities to be responsive to a future that *requires* new solutions for emerging problems. I believe that the solutions should focus on community building, but, in my opinion, the past has led to the creation of educational structures that do not necessarily support this. As a result, the abilities of the parent organizations to deal effectively with the future are limited by the structural organizations that maintain modes of operation that are not conducive to growth. The aim of this book is to establish a base to understand the complexities of the organizational structures. These structures are reflections of the cultures within which reform efforts are directed. Progress needs to legitimize efforts that create and support the conditions for growth for the institutions of professional development of teachers and the environments of learning for students. I would like, in this chapter, to identify the areas of mutual concern to the process of collaboration, particularly those of the creation, support, and effectiveness of forming the transorganizational group. If this group is successful, it must transcend the parent organization's mode of thinking in order to be a learning organization.

What is presented is a creative cookbook that serves as a blueprint for replication of process, not of product. What we learn from the past is how to proceed with the future. Process is about people and how they interact. It is people who create innovations, and it is people who succeed and fail in human endeavors. These same people bring with them a personal history and an institutional history that collectively influence their present behavior, beliefs, and values. The process is like my grandmother's recipes. My grandmother never used a cookbook, never measured an exact amount of anything into her dishes; the ingredients were never combined in the same way since availability was determined by the market on Brighton Beach Avenue in Brooklyn and what the vendors had on their shelves that day. Her creativeness was the constant. The dish always was wonderful, but the observer never knew for sure how the results were achieved. This is similar to collaboration since we cannot be on a systematic quest for the recipe for reform because collaboration is not a concrete set of directions. It is determined first by the participants and the organizational structure. Yet, there are guideposts to direct wise decision making and action. The standard and quality of the recipe is the desired state, even when the ingredients or the players change all the time. It is the mixture of what is available, what is possible, and what is desired at the end that fuels the recipe of reform.

Therefore, the overall purpose of this book is to make sense out of the process of collaboration by analysis and synthesis of information in the field so as to create and sustain collaboration in an environment and between organizations where this is not the norm. Along the way the participants establish new ways of working, assess the reasons for the failure of systemic reform among schools and universities in the past, posit the evolution of structures and vehicles for authentic dialogue, and create new forms of interaction growing out of dissatisfaction with the status quo.

The format for this chapter is to review what we set out to accomplish through the collaborative effort to design, build, and operate a public school on the university campus. The subpurposes clearly emerged throughout the process and related more directly to the two parent organizations and the development and establishment of a group of people who functioned transorganizationally. Analysis of these two organizations led to some issues of methodology of analysis through the elements of building cooperative groups, organizational research, and qualitative approaches of analysis.

Any analysis of the process of forming a collaboration should heed the warnings given as part of the cataloguing of recent innovations and initiatives between universities and school districts. The first caution is that a smorgasbord of reform measures in combination may negate each other. A global perspective on whether initiatives are compatible, possible, or feasible within a setting must be clearly analyzed. What is successful in one place may not be situationally appropriate in another. Next, Olsen (1994, 44–46) stated that there must be the following conditions for success:

• There should be school-level autonomy in decision making, or some structure in place, such as school-based management or shared decision making, that allows decisions to be site specific.
• Commitment by the district and the university for training, resources, support, time, and money should be made and understood up front. The caution is that any of these factors can be used as leverage to influence decisions that are not conducive to programmatic success.
• There should be strong leadership to guide the group and facilitate productive support for the program. For the program to work as intended, Olsen recommended using a coaching model, much like that suggested in the COMER facilitator role, to support training.
• Network support to the parent organizations and to the community at large is another area that must be actively pursued.
• Evaluation of effectiveness when compared to time and costs is an area of contention. The group may have to educate and actively seek a commitment from the parent organizations to understand that the measures for improvement and for research and development may not follow conventional time frames or the academic school year.
• Definitions of success may require altering of perceptions.
• Lastly, quality of program and evaluation should be ongoing and comprehensive, but the focus must remain on improvement.

The following sections are divided into three broad themes. The first theme is centered on the formation and maintenance of interinstitutional and intrainstitutional groups, the formation of a task force, selection of participants, and allegiances to parent organizations through the commitment on both sides to maintain and sustain a collaboration. The second theme involves the understandings held about each participating organization, the cultural world of each organization, and the individual as part of the group, their membership by department, role, and title, and the resultant between-group membership. The resulting organizational analysis was done through qualitative methodology, and the areas to assess include the artifacts, documents, organizational charts, language, myths, sagas, rituals, legends, patterns of behavior, beliefs and values, underlying assumptions, and theoretical constructs as they apply to the project. The third theme is the problems and issues faced by the transorganizational group that are internal and external to the task they are confronting. These elements include the construction of metaphors, leadership issues, and organizational understandings and behaviors.

The final section discusses what remains to be learned about cooperative endeavors and what are the most important issues for practitioners and for organizations. Answers to these questions can provide the vehicle for what we need to know about organizational collaboration that can direct the agenda for future research.

Intergroup and Intragroup Processes
Formation of Areas of Mutual Concern
The need for the establishment of a collaborative environment begins with the recognition that there is a common purpose or goal that could not be achieved or would be made terribly difficult if each of the participating organizations continued to pursue the goals on their own. A clear definition of the mission and goals and the concomitant values and beliefs necessary for the collaboration should be the guiding force for the coming together of representatives from each group. Relating to the Zones of Organizational Involvement described earlier, this is the transition behaviors from Zone I to Zone II to Zone III described in Chapter 7 and depicted in Figure 5.

This clarity of purpose must precede the direction, conceptual framework, and common goal structure of the collective group. It is important to keep the goal in focus at all times because this focus directs the resources needed to organize and complete tasks and clarifies the impediments that deter the end goal. These impediments are both tangible and intangible and as such may be a barrier due to a lack of understanding of what they are.

A collaborative environment includes the need to understand the process of collaboration. The process includes the elements of trust, establishment of clear roles for participants, open communication among and between all participants, tolerance of diversity of opinion and position, and a balance of tasks and assignments between members of each parent organization. Honesty, a spirit of trust and authenticity, candor, and the telling of the truth are important to the success of this process.

The careful assigning of tasks creates an environment in which members of each organization work together in achieving the subtasks of the project. It creates the opportunity for participants to work together in a spirit of honesty and authenticity and to form alliances where they might not ordinarily exist. The roles played by each person in his or her own organization have limitations and restrictions that may be unknown to the other group. This knowledge of how the other organization operates is information that should be shared, but it is usually not shared in a formal manner. This is not just technical information, such as the roles and responsibilities of the titles of participants. It is also not just the legal restrictions that influence decision making. It is the cultural norms, which that are a part of all organizations, to which participants become acculturated. It goes beyond the structural restraints and is the heart of the process of operation that organizations informally instill in their workers. If the transorganization is to evolve, it must be built on the foundations of each of the parent organization's social and cultural norms. These must be understood and respected first.

The environment that is created by mutual consent to accomplish identified goals must engender participation from each of the stakeholders in the project. For this project, the stakeholders were participants in the college of education, teachers in schools, administrators from the college and the public school system, subject area specialists, and representatives from the union. Each came to initial meetings with his or her inherent role definitions and purposes, and the task of the transorganizational group was to establish an environment that promoted continuous ongoing dialogue that would move toward action when appropriate.

To create an environment that is conducive to new ways to solve problems, the argument for change must be made over and over. The reason for the group to form is awareness of the consequences of things staying the way they are. Therefore, alternatives should be the focus of discussion, as well as how to achieve them and plans for organizing. Proceeding to manage and implement the ideas requires an environment of respect and trust. This is important, since identification of the sources of barriers to implement solutions necessitates an understanding of why the barriers exist, what their sources are, who needs to meliorate them, and what is needed to seize the opportunity to make the changes necessary.

Forming and Sustaining a Task Force

Selection of participants is an interesting aspect of forming the collaborative group. Who should be involved does not always produce the mixture that can accomplish the goals and mission of the project. Choices are often made with regard to inclusion rather than expertise, excluding people who could contribute but who do not "get along with" members of the other parent organization. This may be real or perceived; it may be based on past history, past encounter, gossip, or false perceptions. The source may not matter because the perception may be too difficult, complicated, or ingrained to change.

Another problem is full inclusion, or not leaving anyone out, since that may result in constant backtracking. Each meeting is attended by new participants who do not always understand the issues on the table. Each meeting begins with backtracking through old explanations. Inclusion of everyone results in nothing being accomplished that is forward looking since each new person has his or her own agenda and does not see how it fits in or does not fit in to the scheme that is emerging from the group interaction. So, group meetings become educative for new members who, if they join some time after group formation, must be acculturated into the evolving norms of the project.

Another theme that emerges is the perception of the term *expertise*. Since all participants asked to join are presumed to be experts in their fields, the resultant larger group has people with similar expertise in title who, in practice, work, believe, and value in very different ways. These differences create the situation of using the same words but speaking a different language, and clarification of what is meant is important to the creation of mutual understanding. Another related problem is going outside either organization for expertise. This is not always the answer since it does not tap into the resources available within and might be an affront to someone who then pulls out of the process and whose valuable input is lost. Respect of knowledge, experience, and abilities of all the members of the group must be communicated to participants.

In order to proceed once participants are selected, it is necessary to define and mutually structure the roles and responsibilities of the group. An analysis of the work to be done, the sharing of responsibilities, and the definition of individual responsibilities along with the creation of a time frame for accomplishing each task is the next step. Rather than looking at solutions that each parent organization used to solve similar situations in the past, these tasks require new sets of responses that are collaboratively developed. These solutions may require alternate forms of thinking and new problem-solving strategies to produce creative responses that are specific to the goals of the project.

Some conditions can effectively promote this partnership effort. The boundaries of what the participants can accomplish must be understood clearly. Roles and responsibilities should be defined, the work to be done should be mapped out for participants, and a time schedule should be established so that deadlines are met. Meetings should not be dominated by individuals or by one parent organization's members. Altering the site, meeting once on one turf and the next time on the other, seemed to defuse this for our project somewhat. Participants also need to unlearn the positioning of their support by allegiance to their own organization, even when it is at the expense of the project's successful accomplishment of its goals. This occurs over time as the group members create the conditions for decision making that is less tied to parent organization norms. It also occurs as an outgrowth of sharing information and sufficient time to work out collaborative solutions that transcend the parent organizations. This is a function of getting quality information and making that information available, even if no action accompanies it. Justification for position then moves away from cultural norms of the titled roles and organizational power structure toward the creation of mutual concern for solution finding.

Group leadership for collaboration needs to be facilitative. The person facilitating the process needs to involve everyone, keep the focus on goals rather than individual needs, and create the conditions that offer everyone an opportunity to participate fairly. This requires an environment that is fair and consistent so that participants value ideas on their merit and not on their source. Effective leadership balances authority and autonomy, supports skills and abilities of participants, and engenders and seeks input from a variety of sources.

It is important to inform participants constantly of the process and progress of the group. This is true of each group representing the parent organizations as well as for the transorganizational group. The leadership should provide the agenda of meetings in advance to all participants so that there are no surprises at the meeting. Those not able to attend meetings should be kept informed. After each meeting participants should be debriefed as to what happened, what it meant, and why each situation resulted the way it did. This constant analysis between participants maximizes the effective use of time at each larger meeting. It foresees problems and creates opportunities for solutions. In addition, meetings should be geared toward action when possible.

The final point of discussion in this section concerns when to use a group and when individuals would be more effective. This really depends on the task to be done. The project described in this case study established subgroups for the kick-off meeting to work on those areas defined as needing input and buy-in by stakeholders and individuals. We gave the subgroups specific guidelines for dates of completion of their work and defined for them what they were asked to do. They also were asked to keep minutes and submit them to the task force leadership so that coordination and information flow could continue and feedback given so that subgroup work would be efficient and directed toward what was possible. This was effective not only in strengthening the commitment of the parent organizations to the project but also in establishing new linkages that have resulted in other collaborative work between participants from each of the parent groups.

Indicators of Organizational Support and Commitment

Members of the group should understand the group mission, know who the players are and what each wants to accomplish. They should have abilities, skills, and expertise that contribute to group process and the group mission; this includes knowing the limitations, boundaries, and restrictions of what the group is able to accomplish. Participants also must have the time and desire to participate.

In order for a collaboration to be successful, there should be evidence of support from each of the parent organizations. If systemwide policies and practices that stop the collaboration from occurring exist they may have to be altered, waived, or changed to ensure that progress of the group is not deterred. It may also be necessary to eliminate red tape and permission giving, which may be normal operating procedure within the organization. A problem with large bureaucratic structures is often that the permission givers are far removed from the work groups.

Support for mutual group goals should be obtained from the parent organizations, and this may necessitate the realignment of networks between and among each of the parent structures. In the past those elements that have stopped collaboration from occurring may have been structural elements within the organization or people elements that oppose working together because of past history. In this collaboration of a university and a public school system, the support and involvement of the union are essential to the process. For example, one organization may not want certain persons participating from the other organization, or, one organization may include people by virtue of their titles and not their abilities. In any case, there are always people who don't understand why they are not included, and responsibility must be taken by the administration to make it clear to them what the motivation for not including them really is. What you don't want is team members operating out of fear and anger, or sabotaging and spreading rumors where there is no basis.

Time is a crucial element in collaboration—not only the time for completion of tasks, but also the time for participants to listen, attend, and move beyond their own agenda. Task assignments must provide and create the opportunity for team members to learn to work together and become collaborative. This was a primary element of the COMER training described earlier. Participants from both organizations should together attend and talk about implementation both formally and informally. This ability to communicate enhances group process as the interaction becomes self-rewarding. It also keeps a balance of relationships between representatives from each parent organization as the tasks themselves are discussed and carried out collectively.

The infrastructure of both parent organizations must focus on long-term commitment. A view that is bound by concrete time lines and product does not promote the building of a community of information and resource sharing beyond the completion of the product. This view requires the time to identify problems and issues, create institutional or policy changes to implement solutions, and garnish financial resources to implement suggestions. Consideration must be given to rules, regulations, restrictions, union contracts for teacher participation, evaluation, and accountability. Participants also need the support of their parent organization, including a commitment to allot the time to create structures that sustain themselves beyond the project. This includes university support for faculty to participate beyond the service component and school system support to sustain involvement that is time consuming and extends beyond product completion.

Keeping track of the subgroup work and integrating their products into a whole is a large part of the conceptualization done by the task force. This group represents a core of persons from each of the parent organizations who have the ability and authority to make conceptual decisions and formulate, from the input of each of the subgroups, a comprehensive proposal or plan for the project. A useful tool to use once participants are selected and a task force is established is a task time line. This long-term plan should delineate who is involved in each task, what the task to be accomplished is, what the criteria for completion should be, and what decisions the group makes that relate to the task. Actually the task force is responsible for three major sets of plans. First is the direction of the subgroup tasks and the integration of them into an overall plan of action. Second is the transition plan from what is happening now to where the task force wants to go. Last is the results plan, which includes dissemination of results, systemic integration into ongoing operation of each parent organization and sustaining of the collaboration. Evaluation becomes the measure of process as well as product.

The accomplishment of the goals of the project should include the training and further education of people who will carry out the plan. The task force should be aware that implementation must assess the understandings, skills, and dispositions of persons who will be ultimately responsible for carrying out the project; therefore, they must plan for whatever training and skill acquisition is required for this to occur. For this project, COMER training will have to be provided for the school staff, and hopefully this has been built in to the proposal by having a faculty member trained to do this on site and ongoing. This element of retraining must take into consideration the question of how to get people to know what is needed for a particular job they have been doing all along that now requires new skills, which they may not possess.

Trust is a critical component in the establishment of the transorganizational group. One aspect of trust is that participants do what they say they are going to do and that they are consistent and up front with the other members. Being genuine can reduce conflicts that may have contributed to a history of failure in previous attempts at collaboration. The goal is democratic participation and freedom through the reduction or elimination of power and turf that limit collaboration. Trust is built through elements such as no-fault, no-blame discussions and consensual decision making in which participants can openly discuss limitations and restrictions of ideas and find solutions together.

A balance must be established between what is, what each parent organization wants, and what is possible and good for the collective. Balance also must include the element of time—time for each side to present their ideas and to avoid domination by representatives from the other group. Indicators of balance include questions such as the following:

Did they get there on time?

Did they dominate discussion?

Was meeting action oriented or information giving?

Did everyone follow up on commitments?

Was the work of the group representative of one parent organization's norms or that of the evolving culture?

Was the environment of the meetings free of blame and supportive?

Was there evidence of problem solving that was creative, synergistic, and risk taking?

Was decision making consensual or dominated by procedural norms of one group?

Was there evidence of support from both organization's representatives?

Was there evidence of interdependence between groups?

Were needs and requests for information given without being dictated with an air of domination?

Were communications open between groups and were participants available to formally and informally discuss the process?

The created transorganizational group needs full support from the parent organizations. If this full support does not exist, surprises and conditions occur and impede the progress of the task force. In such a case commitments cannot be made with any assurance that they will be carried out because there always will be dependence on the parent organization for resources and authority to continue. This is especially true for the professors who have no obligation or incentive to continue participation in the future. The task force can only create the opportunity, not the reality of ongoing support and involvement.

Organizational Analysis and Methodology Issues

This section discusses how the data was analyzed from this participant observation study. The process for analysis was grounded in qualitative analysis but there are indications that it was the personal quest for sense making that led to the particular emphasis as it appears in the text.

The primary purpose of the analysis was to describe the organizational structures that participants came from and to determine if a true collaborative structure could be created through the resultant transorganizational group. Traditional analysis of the literature on organizations described that of the school system bureaucracy and the university as dissimilar in structure and function. Therefore, attempts at collaboration that do not lead to creating an environment of mutual understanding of how and why each operates within its own environment are transitory and nonsustaining.

Another line of inquiry was that of leadership, change, and resistance to change. The strength of the two organizations described in this study is their sustainability over time. This is also a liability when we try to establish linkages that form relationships for collaboration between them. These two organizations have different operating structures, and the persons selected or elected to participate view the other organization through their own lens. With this come certain assumptions and beliefs about the operations of the other group members. These had to be overcome in order to establish a true collaboration.

What has to be analyzed and how is the analysis done? One of the primary methods is to look and listen, to walk around and observe what occurs, what does not occur, and what cannot occur. Beyond this informal method of collecting information, in order to understand the organization's operations you can look at the documentational artifacts: the records, meeting notes, minutes, organizational charts, and other material products of and about the organization. In addition, the nonmaterial products offer a wealth of information. These include the language used and the patterns of behavior of members, which represent the espoused beliefs and values of participants. The participant observer must keep the information lines open. The gathering and analysis of information can only occur if there is access. This must be an active quest on the part of the observer who should be asking questions about what happened, why it happened, and what does it mean to the project. Only then can synthesis and interpretation occur, with knowledge that full data is available.

The context of the environment the work is done in greatly influences individual behavior. It is, therefore, very important to look for signs of the establishment of a climate and culture of operation that are collaborative and consensual. These signs are found in individual behaviors, events, and the creation of texts, language, and use of a socially constructed world of the collaboration. Counterproductive signs of barriers to this include withholding of time, nonsharing of information, false expectations based on past experience, and organizational structures that really do not allow or permit changes to occur.

The process of analysis is so time consuming that the best advice to the researcher is don't waste time on that which can't be understood or solved. Prioritize what you will analyze and look for those elements that are the most productive lines of inquiry. Those that proved most fruitful for this project included the following:

• Those on the negotiating team had authority for decision making rather than having to take back ideas constantly to the parent organization.
• Internal linkages were established between groups, who then got permission from the parent organizations to negotiate in good faith.
• Organizational and institutional concerns and personal agendas were transcended by common goals.
• People were working from positions of integrity and were willing to share power and change beliefs.
• Time was prioritized on what they were able to do, and there was understanding of some things that were not possible.
• There was an attempt to integrate subgroup and task force work with recommendations for action.

Identifying Problems and Finding Solutions

Metaphors and Descriptors

There is a constant search in analysis of case study material for the metaphors and descriptors that will enlighten the observer with understanding of why events unfold as they do. This is done with selective vision and grounding in a field, with full knowledge of the research methodology used, and in this project, of direct connection to one of the organizations. Rather than describe what you look for in the quest for sense making, what follows are those things that serve to lead the analysis off course:

> Cultural norms are involved in looking for evidence of conspiracy among participants. When two organizations operate in very different ways, what is the norm for one is often not a viable or appropriate means of operation for the other.

> When it all looks too familiar, the time has come to reconsider what appeared to be the rules of operation. Not only does the process have to change, but also the rules of operation.

> Don't blame one organization for the other organization's problems of operation. If the system can't be changed, then look elsewhere or in other directions to implement creative solutions. If tradition, or "that is the way we always do it," dominates the work of the transorganization, the purpose of coming together is subverted and there really is no reason to exist. Keeping lines of communication open and welcoming input from a variety of sources can do much to foster this process.

> It is not always appropriate to go along with the group. Group work is hard. If it is too easy, it is not working correctly. Agreeing is not evidence of loyalty to the parent organization; disagreeing is not being disloyal. It is the dialogue and discussion that lead to progress. If meetings are used only for information giving and products are virtually carbon copies of what is, that is not progress. The transorganizational group should show evidence that a person does not lose by being vocal and being communicative, even if that person is not the leader.

> The last element is a warning to all participants. Don't gossip and tell tales out of group. The group was formed to be process and task oriented. Rumors and half-truths, false perceptions, name calling, and blaming others are all counterproductive.

Leadership

The collaborative transorganizational group must have leadership that transcends each of the parent group organizational limitations.

It is the responsibility of the leadership to keep the focus on the goals and mission while enabling an environment that does not disempower participants. The leadership must also utilize strategies to overcome resistance to new ideas and to direct tasks toward that which can be changed. Since some things are not negotiable or possible to implement, the task of leadership is to direct the group to make their work purposeful. The COMER coach is a good example of facilitative leadership, which effectively utilizes the resources of people, time, materials, funding, and outside support.

Part of the responsibility of leadership is to mediate conflict and keep the focus working toward the goals and purposes of the group. This includes keeping up front the benefits of working together, open lines of input and communication, clarification of needs and expectations of the parent organizations and the community, and establishing a climate of respect and involvement. Thus, when the process is blocked by members, part of the role of leadership is to mediate through the sources of conflict and to align the espoused theories and theories in use so that the organization learns and builds a culture of understanding for itself. This requires that leadership has knowledge beyond that of the formal interactions of the group. This is not underhandedness on the part of the leadership, but a necessity. Remember, knowledge is power coercive for those who withhold it and does not contribute to group processes.

The goal of the collaborative transorganizational group is to solve problems. The effective process of problem solving goes through a five-step process. First, describe what the situation is. Second, state the problem. These steps are separate because interpretation of the situation can be made in multiple frames of reference and solution finding requires that all participants focus on the situation in the same way. Third, what are viable solutions to the problem as stated in step two? Fourth, what criteria will be utilized to select the best solution? Common criteria are cost effectiveness, feasibility of solution, legality, comprehensiveness, and the determination of whether the solution can truly solve the problem. The fifth step is an action plan for implementation identifying who, what, where, and when each task will be done. Of course, it is possible that there are problems that the group cannot solve and the best advice is not to spend time on them. This project had some problems that we dwelled on forever only to find that we really had no say in them—neither in plan implementation nor in alternatives to the way the project had to be done. These included some legal, mandated rules and regulations about schools, lease terms and agreements, and most architectural decisions.

Finally, the group must be kept on course and encouraged to stay current in the literature and research of best practice so that they can make the best decisions about which innovations are viable and not in conflict with others going on at the same time. Team members must have the access or expertise to be reflective and critical of the possibilities for innovation so that all aspects fit together in the overall project and make sense. Leadership must help orchestrate the interconnectedness of ideas and possibilities that are realistic for this project.

Organizational Behavior

The problems and issues of organizational behavior lie with the inability to interpret with surety and then to make predictions based on that analysis. Part of the problem is that we are dealing with people in ever-changing environments, who act in ways consistent with their personal beliefs and values, not necessarily those of the organization itself. Therefore, interpreting all events is important, and data must be kept for later analysis even if the line of inquiry later proves fruitless.

Another area of contention is that of the interactive nature of a profession that should lead to the breaking down of barriers between theory and practice. Problems between and among team members of these two organizations reflect the concern each has for the dual nature of the profession. The university is viewed as being theoretically based, and the school system as practical. Therefore, to describe the organizational behavior of the transorganizational group is to describe the transition to the merging of the rhetoric of theory and practice. This merging was affected both internally and externally in this study by union influence and protection of teacher rights through contracts and negotiations, legal restrictions, and regulatory agency rules.

A large part of the analysis of the transorganizational group revolves around planning and meetings. Regular, effective meetings foster a climate of sharing and support. Meetings create a forum for dialogue; for continuous planning for what action to take, who is to do what, and what resources are necessary; and for establishing criteria for evaluating success. Having a premeeting of our own team to create an agenda for the task force helped move the process along, especially when putting off meeting in the larger group became a critical component in the negotiations.

Prediction and Control

The role of the transorganizational group is to make changes that would not be possible if organizations operated in isolation from each other. The nature of the change may be small, but sufficient to legitimize success. The real change comes about by the alliances and allegiances of members of the two parent organizations working together in the future with new ways to solve problems and create environments for teaching and learning. Therefore, it is all right to make mistakes, but it is not all right to insult and misuse the other group's process.

Success also requires that support be obtained from the larger community to ensure long-term results. The group has to be educated to operate in new ways to solve problems that they have not solved before or were not successful with before in creating long-term change.

Power and Control

There are two sides to power. One view is that power is a negative, that it is used to control people and maintain positions of authority, and that it is self-serving for those who have it. On the other hand, the wise use of power is an aspect of leadership that cannot be underestimated. It is the thing that allows an organization to move forward, to be future oriented, and to be a learning entity. Therefore, the role of the agent of change, which can be a position of power, must be imbued with an ethical outlook to be used for the good.

What needs to be guarded against is the wielding of power through control of agendas, one-sided interpretation for meaning, symbols of success that are not collective, and positioning of personal agendas for personal advancement and organizational status. There can be wise use of power if safeguards exist against its misuse. What is critical is an open information flow with truth telling and full participation—both active and passive, so that all who want to be informed are, even if they say they are not—and full appropriate accountability and quality control.

If efforts are not taken to change the between-organization operation of agencies that are working toward similar goals, the result, as argued previously in this book, is that the efforts are duplicative or do not create the linkages and networks necessary for solutions that need collective skills and resources. It is a problem of being static and repetitive, perhaps even unresponsive to changing societal demands and knowledge about best practice. The effort, however, requires leadership and stewardship to create a facilitative environment to alter the traditional operations of each of the organizations.

The process is arduous, and symptoms of discontent must be dealt with while keeping in focus the goal of the project and the reasons for coming together. These symptoms include the following:

• Extended debate about issues over and over again after they have been put to rest or exhausted.
• Resistance to making creative or innovative changes and over-reliance on the "way that we always do this."
• Factions and support alignments that favor one parent organization over the other without focusing on the problem or issue at hand.
• Pronouncements of information from one side that publicly show off a lack of knowledge of the other.
• Knowledge withholding by one organization which results in power-coercive behavior.

Torn allegiance of a member of one organization for another; often this is seen as empathy for the other side. This often happens when a member of one parent group understands the operating culture of the other and tries to utilize this knowledge to help the transorganizational group advance. This knowledge must be communicated to the group since it can be used to advantage by both organizations.

Another element of power and control is that they often influence by indirect means. For example, the structure of reward at the university is for research, teaching, and service. The impetus to work on a long-term project such as described in this case study requires a commitment on the part of professors that has a great deal of risk imbued in it. The risk is that of utilizing time to participate rather than using time for that which is toward advancement. When you try to engage people in helping with a project such as this, which is a process-oriented rather than product-oriented task, they hold back and do not volunteer their time if other career-advancing tasks have shorter time frames of success. So, people say they are too busy to participate, and they withhold skills, knowledge, and expertise that may be very valuable.

There is also the risk of using up the people who volunteer because they are too able. They can do it all, and they volunteer to do it all; they are too thorough, may take too long, or cannot come through with what they have promised. There must be ownership of responsibility for tasks and the time allotted to do them.

Conclusion

What Remains to Be Learned about Cooperative Endeavors?
Collaboration must be infused with a spirit of cooperation and trust. A sustained trusting environment is one in which people operate from beliefs and values they hold in common rather than from positions that are titled and roles that are standardized. Cooperative projects are creative projects that engage participants in constant problem finding and solution generation. But, the most important part is that they act together to implement solutions in an environment that synergistically meets the changing needs of the community of which they are a part.

What Are the Most Important Issues for
Practitioners and for Organizations?
Rewards and recognition are as important as the work to be done. Genuine support for those who have participated and continue to participate in long-range projects such as these is as important as the work. Sustaining the commitment of one organization to the other is about sustaining interpersonal relationships that are genuine. If we accept the premise that community solutions are to be a part of our future, then we have to be willing to take risks and to realign and reformulate the way we operate and how we work together. Those are the conditions for the community agenda.

Bibliography

Argyris, C. (1990). *Overcoming Organizational Defenses: Facilitating Organizational Learning.* Boston: Allyn and Bacon.

Argyris, C., and Schon, D. A. (1974). *Theory and Practice.* San Francisco: Jossey-Bass.

Barrett, R. A. (1991). *Culture and Conduct: An Excursion in Anthropology.* Belmont, CA: Wadsworth.

Bell, J. S. (1993). Finding the Commonplaces of Literacy. *Curriculum Inquiry.* Vol. 23, No. 2, (Summer): 131–153.

Benne, K. D. (1990). *The Task of Post-Contemporary Education: Essays in Behalf of a Human Future.* New York: Teachers College Press.

Bennis, W. G., Benne, K. D., and Chin, R. (1989). *The Planning of Change.* Ft. Worth: Harcourt Brace Jovanovich.

Blake, R., Mouton, J. S., and McCanse, A. A. (1989). *Change by Design.* Reading, MA: Addison-Wesley.

Blessing, L. (1986). *A Walk in the Woods.* New York: New American Library.

Bolman, L. G., and Deal, T. E. (1991). *Reframing Organizations: Artistry, Choice and Leadership.* San Francisco: Jossey-Bass.

Bolman, L. G., and Deal, T. E. (1992). *Everyday Epistemology in School Leadership: Patterns and Prospects.* Paper presented at the annual meeting of AERA, April.

Bogdan, R. C., and Biklen, S. K. (1992). *Qualitative Research for Education: An Introduction to Theory and Methods.* 2nd Ed. Boston: Allyn and Bacon.

Bourdieu, P. (1993). *The Field of Cultural Production.* New York: Columbia University.

Bullard, P., and Taylor, B. O. (1993). *Making School Reform Happen.* Needham Heights, MA: Allyn and Bacon.

Burns, J. M. (1978). *Leadership.* New York: Harper & Row.

Bushe, G. R., and Shani, A. B. (1991). *Parallel Learning Situations: Increasing Innovation in Bureaucracies.* Reading, MA: Addison-Wesley.

Calhoun, C., Meyer, M. W., and Scott, W. R., eds. (1990). *Structures of Power and Constraint: Papers in Honor of Peter M. Blau.* Cambridge: Cambridge University Press.

Callahan, R. E. (1962). *Education and the Cult of Efficiency: A Study of the Social Forces That Have Shaped the Administration of the Public Schools.* Chicago: University of Chicago Press.

Casti, J. L. (1989). *Paradigms Lost: Tackling the Unanswered Mysteries of Modern Science.* New York: Avon Books.

Chaffee, E. E., and Tierney, W. G. (1988). *Collegiate Culture and Leadership Strategies.* New York: Macmillan.

Chin, R., and Benne, K. D. (1989). General Strategies for Effecting Changes in Human Systems. *The Planning of Change.* Ft. Worth: Harcourt Brace Jovanovich, 22–45.

Cohen, M. D., and March, J. G. (1986). *Leadership and Ambiguity: The American College President.* 2nd Ed. Boston: Harvard Business School Press.

Comer, J. P. (1980). *School Power: Implications of an Intervention Project.* New York: The Free Press.

Conley, S. (1991). Review of Research on Teacher Participation in School Decision Making. In Grant, G., ed. *Review of Research in Education,* Vol. 19, 225–266. Washington, DC: American Educational Research Association.

Darling-Hammond, L., ed. (1994). *Professional Development Schools: Schools for Developing a Profession.* New York: Columbia Teachers College.

Dewey, J. (1939). *Freedom and Culture.* New York: G. P. Putnam's Sons.

Diegmueller, K. (1993). Florida Board Adopts Transition to Accountability System. *Education Week.* February 24.

Dilts, R. (1990). *Changing Belief Systems with NLP.* Cupertino, CA: Meta Publications.

Dittrich, J. E., and Zawacki, R. A. (1981). *People and Organizations: Cases in Management and Organizational Behavior.* Plano, TX: Business Publications.

Etzioni, A. (1975). *A Comparative Analysis of Complex Organizations: On Power, Involvement, and Their Correlates.* New York: The Free Press.

Etzioni, A. (1993). *The Spirit of Community.* New York: Crown.

Frost, P. J., Moore, L. F., Louis, M. R., Lundberg, C. C., and Martin, J., eds. (1991). *Reframing Organizational Culture.* Newbury Park, CA: Sage.

Frost, P. J., Moore, L. F., Louis, M. R., Lundberg, C. C., and Martin, J. (1985). *Organizational Culture.* Beverly Hills, CA: Sage

Flexner, A. (1930). *Universities: American, English, German.* New York: Oxford University Press.

Goodman, P., and Goodman, P. (1960). *Communitas: Means of Livelihood and Ways of Life.* New York: Vintage Books.

Greene, M (1978). *Landscapes of Learning.* New York: Teachers College Press.

Greene, M. (1988). *The Dialectic of Freedom.* New York: Teachers College Press.

Guba, E. G., and Lincoln, Y. S. (1989). *Fourth Generation Evaluation.* Newbury Park, CA: Sage.

Gummer, Burton. (1990). *The Politics of Social Administration: Managing Organizational Politics in Social Agencies.* Englewood Cliffs, NJ: Prentice-Hall.

Hodge, R., and Kress, G. (1988). *Social Semiotics.* Ithaca, NY: Cornell University Press.

James, T. (1991). State Authority and the Politics of Educational Change. In Grant, G., ed. *Review of Research in Education,* Vol. 19, 169–224. Washington, DC: American Educational Research Association.

Kafka, F. (1972). *The Metamorphosis.* Toronto: Bantam Books.

Kanter, R. M., Stein, B. A., and Jick, T. D. (1992). *The Challenge of Organizational Change: How Companies Experience It and Leaders Guide It.* New York: The Free Press.

Konig, R. (Translated by E. Fitzgerald). (1968). *The Community.* London: Routledge and Kegan Paul.

Kuhn, T. S. (1970). *The Structure of Scientific Revolutions.* 2nd Ed. Chicago: University of Chicago Press.

Lanier, J. E., and Little, J. W. (1986). Research on Teacher Education. In Wittrock, M. C., ed. *Handbook of Research on Teaching.* 3rd Ed. New York: Macmillan.

Lieberman, A., ed. (1990). *Schools as Collaborative Cultures: Creating the Future Now.* Hampshire, England: Falmer Press.

Lofland, J., and Lofland, L. H. (1984). *Analyzing Social Settings: A Guide to Qualitative Observation and Analysis.* 2nd Ed. Belmont, CA: Wadsworth.

Malinowski, B. (1944). *A Scientific Theory of Culture.* Chapel Hill: The University of North Carolina.

Marquez, G. G. (1970). *One Hundred Years of Solitude.* New York: Avon Books.

Martusewica, R. A. (1992). Mapping the Terrain of the Post-Modern Subject. In Pinar, W. F., and Reynolds, W. M., eds. *Understanding Curriculum as Phenomenological and Deconstructed Text.* New York: Teachers College Press.

Mason, R. O., and Mitroff, I. I. (1989). A Teleological Power-Oriented Theory of Strategy. In Bennis, W. G., Benne, K. D., and Chin, R. *The Planning of Change.* 4th Ed. Fort Worth: Harcourt Brace Jovanovich.

Newmann, F. M. (1993). Beyond Common Sense in Educational Restructuring: The Issues of Content and Linkage. *Educational Researcher.* Vol. 22, No. 2, March, 4–13.

Olson, L. (1994). Learning Their Lesson. *Education Week.* November 2, pp. 43–46.

Ott, J. S. (1989). *The Organizational Culture Perspective.* Pacific Grove, CA: Brooks/Cole.

Pinar, W. F., and Reynolds, E. M., eds. (1992). *Understanding Curriculum as Phenomenological and Deconstructed Text.* New York: Teachers College Press.

Portes, A., and Stepick, A. (1993). *City on the Edge: The Transformation of Miami.* Berkeley: University of California.

Powell, W. W., and DiMaggio, P. J., eds. (1991). *The New Institutionalism in Organizational Analysis.* Chicago: University of Chicago.

Rosenbach, W. E., and Taylor, R. L., eds. (1989). *Contemporary Issues in Leadership.* Boulder, CO: Westview Press.

Ross, J. (1994). AERA Annual Meeting, April 5. *Advances in the Study of Educational Leadership.* Discussant.

Sackmann, S. A. (1991). *Cultural Knowledge in Organizations: Exploring the Collective Mind.* Newbury Park, CA: Sage.

Saranson, S. B. (1974). *The Psychological Sense of Community.* San Francisco: Jossey-Bass.

Sassen, S. (1991). *The Global City: New York, London, Tokyo.* Princeton: Princeton University Press.

Schwab, W. A. (1982). *Social Consequences and Social Responses to Urbanization in Urban Sociology.* Reading, MA: Addison-Wesley.

Scott, W. R., and Meyer, J. W. (1984). *Environmental Linkages and Organizational Complexity: Public and Private Schools.* Palo Alto, CA: Department of Sociology, Stanford University.

Seashore, S. E., Lawler III, E. E., Mirvis, P. H., and Camann, C. (1983). *Assessing Organizational Change: A Guide to Methods, Measures and Practices.* New York: John Wiley & Sons.

Senge, P. (1990). *Fifth Discipline: The Art and Practice of the Learning Organization.* New York: Doubleday.

Shafritz, J. M., and Ott, J. S. (1992). *Classics of Organizational Theory.* 3rd Ed. Pacific Grove, CA: Brooks/Cole.

Sheive, L. T., and Schoenheit, M. B. (1987). *Leadership: Examining the Elusive.* 1987 ASCD Yearbook.

Sirotnik, K. A., and Goodlad, J. I. (1988). *School-University Partnerships in Action: Concepts, Cases, and Concerns.* New York: Teachers College Press.

Slater, J. J. (1994). An Essay on Community and Freedom: Necessary Ingredients to Collegiality. *Journal for the Art of Teaching,* Florida International University, Vol. II, No. 3, Winter.

Slater, J. J., and Gallagher, J. D. (1994). Micro vs. Macro Planning: Achieving a Balance. *Assessment and Evaluation in Higher Education.* Vol. 19, No. 3, pp. 189–199.

Soder, R. (1994). AERA Annual Meeting, April 5. *School University Human Services Partnerships.*

Srivastra, S., Cooperrider, D. L., and Associates. (1990). *Appreciative Management and Leadership: The Power of Positive Thought and Action in Organizations.* San Francisco: Jossey-Bass.

Stallings, J. A. (1991). *Connecting Preservice Teacher Education and Inservice Professional Development: A Professional Development School.* ED 339682.

Stallings, J. A. (1992). *Lessons Learned from a Four-Year Case Study of Preparing Teachers for Inner-City Schools.* ED346230.

Teachers of the Twenty-First Century: Blueprint 2000 Teacher Accomplished Practices. (1994). Educational Standards Commission, Florida Department of Education, Tallahassee, Florida, July 1.

Whitehead, A. N. (1954). *The Aims of Education.* New York: New American Library.

Index